Golf for Life

How To Get It and How To Keep It
Stories From the Tee

KIM ANDERS, PGA

Cover Design by 100Covers.com
Interior Design by FormattedBooks.com

ISBN: 978-1-7356824-1-9 (Paperback)
ISBN: 978-1-7356824-0-2 (EBook)

THANK YOU FOR BUYING MY BOOK!

To show my appreciation I want to give you some special bonus information about how to approach golf if you feel like it is just too complex, or you have too much to think about, or too many areas in need of attention.

Your Plan will help you organize what you need most, and help you focus on these areas.

Next, is more information to further support using Soft Hands, and how 'Listening to Your Clubs' will enable you to know immediately when you start getting a little off, and need to fix before it becomes a big problem.

Just go to this site to download your additional information:
https://mailchi.mp/3144c07642f3/golf-for-life

I hope this information and my book help you as much as it has helped the people in my schools.

To better golf, fairways and greens,
Kim

DEDICATION

This book is dedicated to all the students I have worked with over the years. You have inspired me to be a better coach, and given me enough material for this book and probably a few more.

A special thank you to my wife, Heather, who has been with me through all the unique and trying and wonderful times in my career as a golf professional. And for encouraging me to put this book together.

We hope you enjoy it, and are a better player having read it.

MY FAVORITE GOLF QUOTE

"If people gripped a knife and fork the way they do a golf club, they'd starve to death."

Sam Snead

CONTENTS

INTRODUCTION

This Book is for Golfers:

Those Who Almost Can, and Those Who Want to Learn

GOLF IS ADDICTING. All it takes is one swing, where *it* all comes together and the ball flies further than ever before. *It* was effortless. All the awkward moving parts and positions finally came together to produce a perfect shot. Instantly, you are hooked!

You think, *How did that happen? What was I thinking about? I don't remember. Why can't I remember what I did just a few moments ago? I just hit one of the best shots of my life and I don't have a clue as to what I did or how* it *happened! What's wrong with me?*

Quick, get another ball out so I can do it *again before the magic leaves my body. Focus on everything I have read and heard so I can repeat that perfect swing I just made*

The ball flies wildly over the fence, never to be seen again. *I can get* it *back. Give me another ball. I know* it *is there because I just did* it. *Sadly,* it *is gone. The problem is I don't know where* it *went.*

Give me another ball. I'm not quitting till I get another good one! I have to finish with a good shot. I wonder what time the sun goes down and it gets dark!

I've seen this scenario hundreds of times. I've heard my students and members tell me their stories thousands of times. Change the name but the story is the same.

I have been a golf professional for over 40 years. I'm a Life Member of the PGA of America. I have given thousands of lessons, most on the lesson tee and golf course, but also in living rooms, backyards, parking lots, on ski slopes, and I've even drawn a few small crowds in bars.

Over the years I have written about 150 articles for a regional publication in the Southwestern US and received a generous amount of positive feedback from the readers.

I'm told I have a somewhat different approach to golf. My methods have been very successful for my students, both on and off the course. Many have said things like, "Once I could implement your teachings for the course, I was able to apply them to other areas of my life, and they improved too!"

My reason for compiling these articles is to help golfers improve their game. I want people to realize what is important and what isn't when they swing a golf club. What they should think about and how to avoid the mistakes we all make.

Every article contains a message most golfers will be able to relate to. Some of the messages are similar, just worded differently. Teachers do that. We repeat ourselves. We say the same thing in different ways, hoping something will stick somewhere in our student's brain.

We will continue to make mistakes when we play. The key is to keep our mental lapses to a minimum, to play within ourselves, and to have more discipline.

If you can do this just a little bit you WILL play better, and you will enjoy the game much more.

Why not?

The Locker Room

For about 10 years I wrote articles for my dear friend who published the *Arizona Golfer Magazine*. Frequently, readers would contact me to say thank you for the helpful tip, or how they had laughed out loud because I had perfectly described one of their playing partners.

After a few years I began getting requests to put together a collection of my articles. As I was putting this book together I quickly realized as a golf coach it didn't really make sense to draw attention to the problems golfers commonly have with the game, and not offer some solutions.

So, I added *The Swing* section after the stories. It's not the light reading found in the articles, but if you want to get more serious and technical, and discover how to correct a problem you're having, you should be able to find your fix there.

Better Golf—How To Find It and How To Keep It.

PRACTICING

Practice Makes Perfect, Right?

THE PGA TOUR LatinoAmerica Qualifying Tournament is here this week and many of our residents have been out following the players and watching them practice. This has prompted a lot of interesting questions and comments.

Comments have included, "These guys really swing hard," "They sure practice a lot," "Their muscle memory is incredible," and "This proves practice makes perfect!"

Let's start with the idea that practice makes perfect. Practice does not make perfect. Practice makes permanent! Perfect practice makes perfect.

Does your practice session involve getting a couple of large buckets of balls, heading to the practice tee and starting to go through a checklist of exercises and thoughts you recently heard or read about? If one idea doesn't work, you move on to the next one on the list until you find the magic tip that works for you?

When you practice, do it with a purpose, a plan. Consider about 40 or 50 balls for a practice session, not a couple hundred. Start with some practice swings—a lot of practice swings—using the moves or positions you want to be doing.

Watch your shadow. If your shadow looks good you probably look good. When you start hitting balls, looking good and focusing on what you wanted to work on is most important. Where the ball goes is of little importance.

Hit a few balls making sure you evaluate what you have done, good or bad, on each swing. Then make some more practice swings, correcting any aspect of your swing you didn't do properly.

If your swing feels good don't mess with it. The problem is more likely to be in your setup, grip, or some part of the swing you haven't addressed.

A good practice session involving 50 balls should last at least 45 minutes if done properly. Practice properly! Quality practice not quantity practice. Lots of practice swings, lots of thought about what you are doing and what you want to be doing.

Hitting hundreds of balls only cements what you are doing—it doesn't make your swing perfect, it makes your swing permanent. Practicing is a lot of work and can be mentally exhausting. When your brain gets tired or you lose your discipline you are done. I don't care if you've only hit 20 balls, you are done.

And finally, tour players swing faster than most of us, not harder. They practice with a purpose. Muscles don't have memory. Your brain has memory, so train it to make good swings. You'll be surprised how much your game improves!

Putting Problems? Move the Hole!

How many times have you had a downhill putt you knew was very fast and you only hit your first putt about halfway to the hole? Or, you're faced with an uphill putt and you end up blowing it way past the hole, leaving you with a tricky little downhill four-footer?

This happens because you are allowing your brain to dictate how you stroke the ball. Unfortunately, as remarkable as the brain is, it doesn't know how to putt a golf ball.

Here's how the brain works. The brain sees all putts as though they are flat, at least until the last moment, when it's too late. Your brain knows the ball is 14 feet 6-½ inches from the hole. You set up to the ball and pull the trigger. The brain and body take over, which is just what you want. You are allowing your body to do what you have trained it to do.

A long smooth stroke, keep the putter moving through the ball towards the hole… You draw the putter back to hit the ball exactly 14 feet 6-½ inches and then it happens! Your brain finally kicks in and says, *Wait, this is REALLY FAST so hit it easy!* You do your best to slow the putter down so you don't blow the ball way past the hole. You know the feeling. It's like driving your car with one foot pressing on the accelerator and the other foot pressing on the brake.

Or, in the case of an uphill putt your brain says, *Wait a minute. This is going to be slow so you need to hit it hard.* How can you hit it harder when you only took the club back far enough to move the ball 14 feet 6 ½ inches in the first place? Here's how.

You jab it up the hill to compensate for not taking the club back far enough to have it go the distance you wanted up the hill. You watch the ball speed past the hole and finish about 4 feet beyond where you wanted it to go. Now you have a slick downhill putt coming back and a bad attitude is piloting your stroke. Your brain tells you a four-putt is not out of the question!

The next time you are on the practice green try this. Find a spot that would be a fast downhill putt and play a couple of balls to this hole. Do you feel yourself putting on the brakes so you don't hit it too far? Next, pick a spot that is half or a quarter of the way to the hole. This is the target I want you to putt to.

You may have a 10-foot putt but you mentally move the hole to a point just 2 feet away. This way you take the putter back to hit the ball 2 feet. You put a good 2-foot stroke on the ball and allow the slope of the hill to take the ball the extra 8 feet to the hole.

Don't change your stroke to compensate for the slopes you'll encounter on the greens. Keep the same stroke and just move the hole so your brain works for you, not against you.

This may be the least scientific approach you'll ever hear when it comes to golf. But a little practice moving the hole around can pay off big time on the scorecard!

Are 4 Clubs Better Than 14?

Some of the players at our course must feel golf is too easy using their full set of clubs, because they have taken to playing with only 2 or 3 clubs and a putter. And you know what? Most are finding they are scoring better than they do with all 14 clubs. Why is this?

I subscribe to the theory that we should try to use one swing all the time and simply switch clubs to the one that goes the desired distance. Sounds pretty good, and after all, most manufacturers build irons in sets of seven to eleven clubs—I'm guessing they do this for a reason. One swing, clubs designed to go different distances. Hmm... But, over the years I have seen so many people playing better with fewer clubs, I wondered, could there be something to this?

In order to test this theory I went out last week with a driver, 6-iron, sand wedge, and putter. At first it was tough because I was missing the majority of my clubs. But after a few holes I started thinking better, planning on where I wanted the ball to finish, using strategy, and creating different shots. High soft fades, driver off the fairway to somewhere around the green so I could use my sand wedge to chip it close. It was a new experience even though I had done this many years ago.

What did I say? Was it, "I started thinking better, planning... using strategy...creating!"? Maybe there is something to leaving 10 clubs in the trunk. It reminded me of when we used to try to hit different shots around trees, see how close we could get to a hedge and still get the ball over it, or how low we could hit a 9-iron.

I ended up playing pretty well, at least better than I had expected. It was a different game just having 4 clubs to choose from. But even then I still had club choices to make several times, because there were different shots I could create with the few clubs I had.

It's not like I was trying to figure out if I should hit a hard 8 or an easy 7. I was caught between hitting a driver from 225 yards, hopefully landing near the green but maybe in the rough, or sand; hitting a little 6-iron short and in the fairway, leaving a ¾ sand wedge; or just hitting 2 full sand wedges and being home. The 6-iron/sand wedge combo won out and I birdied that particular hole.

Many people think a 3 or 4 club event is silly and a waste of time. But, if you take the time to try it you may find it helps your entire game because you must plan and create and think your way around the golf course, rather than simply pulling out the correct club and swinging it with little thought as to what you really want to do.

And, you may find 4 clubs really do work better than all 14.

Spice up Your Practice—Play Situation Golf

When you go to the practice range do you find yourself getting bored? Golf is almost always easy on the range. I hit the ball close to the hole at least 90% of the time on the range. I hit soft fades and draws, control trajectory—the game just isn't that tough. It's when you move 25 yards over to the first tee that the game gets hard.

Let's take a look at the typical driving range. Most are 50 to 100 yards wide or even more, with numerous greens, flags and signs, etc. I think most golfers are pretty confident they can hit a fairway with any club when it is 50 yards wide! And with half a dozen targets to shoot at you are bound to get close to one of them at some point during the shot.

Next time you go to the practice facility try playing what I call Situation Golf. Give yourself situations you come across when you are playing. Design your own holes on the practice range. *Left of that tree is water, and to the right of the yellow flag is out of bounds.* Now let's see you hit it in the fairway.

Or, give yourself a shot to an island green 140 yards away, using your 140- and 150-yard clubs. Hit your wedge to an area where you have designed, or imagined, a green with bunkers front and left, but open right and long. Use a lone golf ball or a cluster of golf balls already on the range to define how far you need to carry the ball, or the maximum distance a shot should go.

Once you have mastered that hole, design another hole. One with problems on the opposite side of the hole you just finished practicing on. Design holes that play to your strengths, and then create some that emphasize situations that are more difficult for you.

There aren't many straight golf holes. Even the straight holes have some characteristics the architect included that give straight holes nice motion, as if the hole did turn a little one way or the other.

When you practice don't just work on the straightaway layout of the practice area. Create your own fairways, greens, and hazards. Design one hole playing to the back left corner of the range, then go to the back right with the next.

One of my favorites is if a tree or flag marked the left edge of the fairway for one of my holes, I use it to mark the right edge of the fairway on the next hole. You'll be surprised how tough it can be to hit the ball to a place you had designated as trouble a few minutes earlier.

Put some fun and variety into your practice sessions by designing your own holes and play Situation Golf. You may find you handle the real situations a lot better the next time they come up on the golf course.

Good Shots, Bad Direction?

It seems I've been on a roll lately with some of my students. I think 5 or 6 of the last 10 people I've worked with have had a similar problem. Instead of wanting help so they could hit the ball longer, straighter, higher, or something, they asked for assistance because they felt they weren't hitting the ball where they aimed, or at least, where they wanted it to go.

That's a fair request. Doesn't seem like it should be that tough to fix. So I watch Bill hit a few shots and I'm pleased to see he has been working on what we did the last time we were together. He was hitting a short iron and balls were consistently landing within 4 or 5 yards of his target. For a 15 handicapper from 125 yards, I am pleased with his progress.

Then I notice he starts changing his setup followed by several little swing changes. The solid swing he was using five minutes ago has been replaced with a bunch of mechanical motions that have little functionality when it comes to hitting a golf ball.

"Bill, what the heck are you doing?" I ask.

He says, "This is what I was talking about. I'm hitting the ball all over the place."

A few minutes ago he was making nice swings and hitting consistent shots. Now he's become very mechanical and forced with his movements.

As it turns out, it's not that Bill isn't happy with his shots landing within 4 to 5 yards of his target. It's that one shot is 4 or 5 left and the next 4 or 5 right! He thinks he's spraying it all over the place. Obviously Bill, the 15 handicapper, doesn't understand how difficult this game is!

Bill likes the way his swing feels, makes solid contact, gets good ball flight, and has a lot of consistency. But, he seems to feel he should hit the ball closer to the hole than he does, even though he isn't exactly the club champion. Bill is fairly typical, in that he feels a good swing that produces good ball flight should also go exactly where he wants it to go. Regardless of where he aimed.

This is what I tell my students: If you like the way it feels and the flight, regardless of where it goes, you are moments from greatness. DO NOT change your swing in an effort to make the ball go where you want it to go.

If you like the feel and flight but wonder why it is going over there, check your alignment.

After hitting a ball, put your feet down where you started and then take your club and put it up against your heels (your heels will give a more accurate representation of your alignment than your toes).

Odds are very good your club is pointed pretty close to where your ball went, or at least where it started. If the club is pointed at your target, hold it across your hips and then your shoulders to see if you are lined up properly.

When you practice, use a couple of clubs on the ground to help get a feel for better alignment. One club should be 4 to 6 inches on the far side of the ball and pointed at your target. Place the other club parallel to the first but near your feet. Make sure your feet are an equal distance from the second club, and you feel like your shoulders and hips are parallel to both these clubs. Now you should be well aligned for your shot.

Alignment can be tough to check by yourself, but it can be done. Before you go and change your swing make sure you are set up to the ball properly with the feet, hips, and shoulders all aligned at or a little left of your target.

Have No Time to Practice? Sure You Do!

Life is busy! Between work, shuttling kids around, looking after the yard, and everything else we have to do, when do we have time to practice our golf game? Time is limited so you'll be happy to know you don't have to get in the car and drive to the course and spend 30 minutes or more on the practice tee—just practice at home!

Five or ten minutes of Shadow Golf can do far more good than a bucket of balls or playing 9 holes. And I'll bet it's a lot more productive than either one of them.

When you get home grab a club and go out in the yard and position yourself so the sun is at your back and you are facing directly towards your shadow. Mornings and evenings are perfect for this because your shadow will be longer and it will be easier to see what you are doing. Make a few swings and watch your shadow.

Like a video, your shadow doesn't lie. You can also face a full-length window and watch your reflection. If you can make your shadow or reflection look good you will look good. Does your setup look like the players on the Tour? Watch your head to make sure there isn't too much movement to the right on the backswing.

Look at your right hip. Does it move to the right on the backswing or stay where we want in about the same place as it started? Does your right knee move to the right on the backswing or do you keep it where it was at the start of the swing (I hope)? Can you make your right hip or knee initiate the downswing?

Now turn sideways to see what your setup and swing looks like from that angle. This exercise allows you to see what you really look like without worrying about where the ball is going. Let's face it—we're all far too concerned with where the ball goes and not what makes it get there.

By watching your shadow you will build "good looking" swings and become much more aware of what your body is doing. This awareness and repetition will translate to more consistent swings and shots. Even if your shots aren't going where you want, they will have become more consistent. I'd much rather see the same swing flaw consistently than a new swing every time you pull the trigger.

This is a great exercise that will do more for your game than a barrel of practice balls. Why not get the whole family out in the yard for a 10-minute round of "Shadow Golf"? After all golf is a family game, and it is A Game For Life!

Don't Get Mad—You're Not That Good

I get tired of people bringing broken clubs in to be fixed, saying they accidentally hit a tree or rock, tripped over it, ran the cart over it, it got stuck in the bag when they were pulling it out, the twins were having sword fights... Forget the excuses. You lost your temper over your golf game and broke a club. Pretty silly when you consider you aren't that good!

Golf is a leisure sport. We do it for fun, for relaxation, to get away from the stressful world we live in. And what happens? We end up getting so upset we develop ulcers, lose sleep, and worst of all, while we're on the course doing all this relaxing we have temper tantrums. We slam our clubs into the ground, sometimes repeatedly until they break, and on occasion we even use questionable language.

Why do we let this game do that to us? I doubt there are any tour players who will read this book, but they are about the only ones I can think of who have any right to be upset with their golf game. They make their living playing golf. It is their job. They deserve to get upset from time to time.

But do they? Rarely. The best in the world, who take this game more seriously than anyone, almost never let their frustrations get the best of them. For them, a missed putt can mean thousands of dollars, maybe hundreds of thousands of dollars.

So why do the tour professionals take a missed 5-footer in stride and we non-tour players seem to think we should make 100% of these putts? We expect to always hit our approach shots next to the hole, never go out of bounds or in a hazard. And when something does go against us we react like a child that's been denied candy at the checkout stand.

Let's face it—we're not that good. We have no business getting upset about our golf games. Golf is incredibly difficult. The best players in the world frequently hit bad shots. Most of us 'normal people' spend little time practicing and when we do play our mind is frequently on something else of higher priority.

Look at it this way. You have one year to prepare for a special round of golf. Your bills and family are taken care of, and your only responsibility is to practice and play in preparation for this one round. The only thing you know for sure is you are going to hit some good shots and you're going to hit some bad shots. That's it! Hit some, miss some! That's golf. Get over it.

Once I realized I'm not that good I started enjoying this wonderful game a lot more. Bad shots don't tear my heart out because I now understand they are just part of the game. I've seen Tiger and Rory hit quite a few bad shots, by anyone's standards.

If they can hit bad shots and not explode I guess I can too. I can hit a lot of bad shots and it's OK, because golf is hard and I'm just not that good.

Practice What is Important

I played the other day with one of my young members who is about a 10 handicap but swears he is a 3, it's just that the handicapping system isn't fair to good players. Say what? I couldn't wait to hear this one!

He proceeded to tell me what a strong player he was due to his distance off the tee, distance with his fairway woods (metals), and distance with his irons. I guess all he was lacking was distance with his short game and putter.

However, he did manage to show me some impressive distance around the greens a few times that day. Unfortunately, he wasn't going for distance at the time. He just happened to hit the ball right in the middle of the forehead and send it about 70 yards when he only wanted 17.

Anyone who has been around our course for any length of time is well aware of his practice sessions. Here's how they go: Get 4 buckets of balls (about 60 balls each), warm up with 6 wedge shots and then move straight to the driver for the remaining 234 balls.

I asked why he doesn't spend more time on his short game and learned, "The short game is no fun to practice." I asked him how much fun he had taking 3 or 4 to get down from around the green. "I was just a little off today."

Well, not that I was counting, but of the 11 greens he missed by 10 yards or less, it took him 3 strokes to get in the hole 6 times, 4 to get in 4 times, and 5 strokes once. He didn't get 'up and down' once. Not once in 11 attempts. Even for a 10 handicapper that's not very good!

The first professional I ever worked for told me about the birthday present his mother had given him when he was fairly new to the game. One hundred golf lessons (for $400). The thing that made this story stick with me all these years, aside from the fact that you could ever get a lesson for $4, was that in those 100 lessons he never hit a ball more than 50 yards. His golf coach told him that you win tournaments on and around the green, not with the big clubs.

And he was right. My boss was one of the top players in the state. We used to say you could put a ball anywhere in the clubhouse and as long as someone held the doors open, he would find a way to get the ball in the hole on the 18th green in 2 shots. And most of the time he would.

Hitting a golf ball a short, precise distance may not be as exhilarating as having people ooh and aah over your soaring drives. But, if you adopt the right attitude and make your short game a priority, you may find you receive far more recognition than the guys who put on the exhibitions on the range with their long drives.

PLAYING

Use Soft Hands to Hit It Hard

HAVE YOU EVER wondered why your hard swings hit shots that rarely go very far and are usually offline, whereas your smooth 'just get it out there somewhere' swings frequently hit the ball 20 yards further than usual and right down the middle? It's probably because you have "soft hands" on the smooth swings, which allows you to release the club properly.

A good way to get the feel of "soft hands" is to swing the club back and forth from waist high on the backswing to waist high on the forward swing. Make sure the toe of the club is pointing roughly up at the sky when it reaches waist high on both back and forward swing. As you swing back and forth you want to hold on just tight enough to avoid losing the club, moving smoothly through the changes of direction. If it feels loose, sloppy, and out of control, you're probably doing it right.

Notice how your hands roll over at impact. They will roll over just because the club is accelerating under its own weight through the ball, not because you are making them turn over.

This all happens automatically by relaxing the hands and arms on the downswing, rather than creating tension by trying to physically hit the ball. I use this exercise all the time when I'm playing to remind my hands of what I want them to do.

Now take some full swings at one-half to three-quarter speed. Make sure you still feel the hands release through the hitting area. Once you have this down you can start hitting balls.

Keep in mind, no matter how good your "soft hands" are at address, when you get to the top of your backswing and start down there's a good chance you'll be choking the life out of the club. Try relaxing your grip pressure as you start the downswing to regain your "soft hands." Trust the club to find its way to the ball. The worst thing you can do is try to guide the club to the ball.

Golf is about controlling the golf ball. The way you control the golf ball is by giving up control of the golf club, which is done by using soft hands. Most people try to control the golf club, which results in losing control of the ball. You can only control one of them, and the club is not the one you want to focus on.

You spend a lot of money on your golf equipment. It is packed with technology and knows how to hit a golf ball perfectly every time. It will take wonderful care of you if you just trust it and let it do what it is built to do.

Don't mess with perfection! You have enough to do just being smooth and maintaining your soft hands. Once you get the feel for this you'll find both your good and bad shots will go a lot longer and straighter.

No Magic Pills in Golf

I was working with one of my members last week and she said, "I need a magic pill I could take that would give me more discipline when I play golf." This got me thinking, not about coming up with a magic pill, but about what's the real problem students have in the learning process.

I've found this is a huge issue for many other golf coaches out there as well. Our students struggle with their game until they can't stand it anymore, and are forced to ask us for help.

They spend their hard-earned money for one or multiple sessions, during which the "light goes on" and they feel their swing. The ball flies further and irons stop quicker. Their "splatter patterns," or bad shots, are much tighter and going longer and straighter than before. And all this happens with an easier swing.

So why doesn't all this good stuff stick with them? I've gone through stages when I felt I must not have left my students with the tools they needed to keep the good swings going; on the other hand, sometimes I felt maybe I had given them too many tools.

I finish each session with assigning two things to think of. One, Two. Add a couple of exercises to keep One and Two working, and that's it. What was I missing?

The following day I was working with a player off the PGA LatinoAmerica Tour. He said he wasn't playing badly, but he just couldn't get comfortable with his swing. He said, "It feels like the wheels could fall off at any time." His swing looked good but he just didn't feel comfortable with it.

I asked what he didn't like about each swing and his comments were, "I held on too much," or "I had a little too much or too little [of something]." He couldn't quite figure it out, and I was having trouble diagnosing what was causing his insecurity. He could still shoot under par but it wasn't a comfortable swing for him.

We took a break and I asked him why he felt he was doing too much or too little, but he couldn't really explain why these bad feelings were happening. After a long pause he said, "I'm ball bound. The ball has taken control of me!" That's when the 'light turned on' for me.

He went on to recite to me everything we had previously worked on, the exercises I had given him to use when he practiced and when he was playing. He showed me in slow motion the mechanics we had worked on, and they were perfect.

I didn't say a thing. The light had turned on for me, and it had just turned on for him too. He said, "I've lost my discipline!" Yup, he had! "I'm focused on the ball instead of what I'm doing."

Everyone does this from time to time. All the players I work with at this level have good mechanics. The problems they usually have are related to the fact that they are constantly striving to improve, and in the process they end up changing something that is good.

If this happens to you, think back to something your golf coach gave you that worked. If you don't have a coach go get one. A good coach will make the game of golf a lot more fun and a lot easier.

Just the magic pill you were looking for!

One Swing for Every Club?

How many times have you heard someone say, "You need to swing the long clubs just like you do your 7-iron"? This sounds good in theory but it just doesn't make sense. After all, you can't possibly swing a driver like a pitching wedge and expect it to go 100 to 150 yards further like it's supposed to. Can you?

The equipment manufacturer's goal is to make the game easier and more enjoyable, not more difficult. All those clubs we have in our bag are there to help us, not to make the game more challenging.

But, sometimes it is confusing. Should I hit a 7 or an 8? If you only had the odd numbered irons it would be a lot easier. You would hit the 7 because there's no way a 9 would ever get there. But, this causes another problem.

How do you hit a 7 the distance an 8 would go? Just swing easier I guess. Notwithstanding what I said earlier about being able to play an interesting game with a limited number of clubs, I'm probably better off having the full set of clubs.

The reason we have all those clubs in our bag is because they are all built to go certain distances, WITH THE SAME SWING. Now technically it really isn't the same swing, but we certainly don't try to make a different swing with different clubs.

It's a different swing because of the shaft length. With the short clubs we are bent more at the waist, or hips, which limits the amount of shoulder and hip turn we can have, and gives us a more upright swing plane. This is a good thing because a swing with a pitching wedge is not a power swing. It's a more controlled swing designed to produce a more accurate result.

The "long clubs" have longer shafts so we can stand up taller. This enables us to make a fuller shoulder turn which translates into more clubhead speed and more distance.

Unfortunately, this also translates into a greater margin for error. It's like how driving slowly makes it easier to keep your car on the road than driving fast. You just can't do them both and expect great results all the time.

You see, it's not so much that we are using the same swing as we are not trying to use different swings. You have 14 clubs in the bag; one is a putter. If you had a specific swing for each club you would need 13 swings just to hit the ball at all. Add 13 more to draw the ball, another 13 to fade it, 13 each for low and high shots…. And, you're still a long way from playing like a tour player!

I know Tiger has more than one swing as do the rest of the guys and gals on the Tours. I even have 2 or 3 swings I put to use during a round. But I can tell you 90% of the time my thought is to make the same old swing, again and again.

The game of golf is just too difficult to have different swings for different clubs. You'll be a lot better off using the same swing, or swing thoughts, and letting the clubs do the rest.

Use the Right Tempo for Your Personality

I understand the new player asking about what their swing tempo should be, but I'm always surprised at how many experienced players ask whether they should change their tempo to swing faster or slower.

Tempo is very important in the golf swing, but generally not something you want to mess with too much. Just be aware of what yours is. Why? We all have a natural tempo that is personal to each of us. This is always preferable to trying to copy someone else, thus forcing an unnatural tempo.

Our swing tends to change when the pressure is on. Most players' swings get shorter and quicker when the pressure is on. Once you are aware of your personal tempo, it is easier to recall when you are under pressure and avoid falling apart when it really counts.

I have a friend who can't sit still. Everything he does is fast, including his golf swing. Start to finish, his swing only takes about half a second, and maybe less. I know I'll never get him slowed down, but when he does slow down just a little he plays much better.

As for me, I have a fairly slow personal tempo. I walk slowly, talk slowly, eat slowly. I use the excuse that with a 36-inch inseam I don't have to move my legs very fast to keep up with everyone else. Actually, I just have a slower personal tempo and rhythm than most people. My golf swing takes more than 1-¼ seconds to complete.

How do you find your personal tempo? Pay attention to how your body moves when you walk somewhere. Not when you're late and need to get there quickly, but when you're just moving from one place to another. Do you use shorter strides and a quick pace, or do you make long, slower strides?

When you speak, do people have trouble staying awake because your delivery is so slow, or are they wondering how you manage to talk without ever taking a breath? These are going to be good indicators of what your personal tempo is, and what the tempo of your golf swing will be.

Regardless of whether you have a slow, medium, or fast personal tempo, using the one that comes naturally will be more productive, comfortable, and repeatable than one requiring a great deal of thought to manufacture.

However, that being said, I have never seen an overly fast swing that held up well under pressure. If you're going to err with your swing speed, or tempo, I would recommend you err on the slow side. A slower tempo allows many of the necessary mechanics of the swing to take place in proper sequence, whereas a faster tempo generally requires overuse of the muscles in the hands and forearms, which is not something you want.

The club goes back and then it comes down. Back and down. One, Two. That's it! There is no Three in a golf swing, just One, Two. By the time your swing gets to Three you are either patting yourself on the back or reaching in your pocket for another ball.

Use Your Stock Shot More

I've been working with a young man who wants to go to the PGA LatinoAmerica Tour qualifying tournament in a couple of months. He strikes the ball great on the practice tee—has all the shots—but is having trouble taking it to the golf course.

We head out on the course and I watch him play four holes. As it turns out he is trying to work, or turn, the ball on every shot. I don't want him to be working the ball all the time, I want him to be using his stock shot at least 80% of the time—more if he's not comfortable working the ball at that moment.

He plays those four holes two over. I tell him all I want him to do the rest of the round is hit his natural shot. He is three under par the next five holes. He tells me he has decided to play his stock shot all the time, but will continue to practice working the ball till he becomes more comfortable with it. Pretty good idea, I think!

In the case of my guy, he didn't have a 'go to' shot, or a stock shot, when he came to me. He now realizes what type of ball flight his swing naturally produces. He has a stock shot that, when the pressure is on, is the shot he uses. It is a swing that is simple for him, repeatable, and he knows where the ball is going to go.

He felt that in order to be a good player he needed to be able to work the ball, which is true. However, at this stage of his career he needed a stock shot more than he needed to 'move' the ball on every shot.

We all have a stock shot, and if you don't, I suggest you get one—soon! The stock shot is just that; it's the shot you use the majority of the time. It is the shot your swing naturally produces. It is dependable. It is an old friend that won't let you down.

I used to play a lot of golf with a guy that played to a +3 handicap, which means his average score was in the mid to high 60s. There wasn't much I liked about his game other than the way he could get the ball in the hole, which is pretty important.

For example, he averaged at least 320 yards off the tee using a 12-degree shallow face driver with a regular shaft. He would set up and aim about 35 to 40 yards right of where he wanted the ball to go, and then on the downswing he would redirect his swing path and pull the shot back to the desired target line. And, he absolutely smashed the ball.

It doesn't matter if your stock shot is high or low, moves left to right, or right to left, as long as you know where it is going.

This is an area of your golf game where you can think like the tour professionals. Don't try a lot of low-percentage shots—those shots you know you have little chance of pulling off. Develop a stock shot you can pull out of your bag anytime—it's your money shot!

Use your stock shot more and watch your scores come down and your level of enjoyment go way up!

Tight Goes Right

I've heard a lot of suggestions as to how tightly, or softly, we should hold the golf club. And I've probably used many of them myself trying to get my students to let the club do its work instead of working the club.

Hold the club like a bird, a ripe banana, your girlfriend's hand. Well, this is all great in theory but when trying to inflict as much damage as possible on the golf ball, we have all killed a lot of birds, squished a lot of bananas, and broken our girlfriend's hand many, many times.

It's easy to have soft hands at address, when the club is resting on the ground, and we have yet to begin the assault on the ball. We might even have a soft grip from the ball to the top of the backswing. But when we get to the top of the backswing everything seems to change. It's at this point the 'genetic creator of bad golf shots,' the kill gene, kicks in. Our total focus is punishing the ball as severely as we possibly can.

The top of the backswing is when we should be holding the club like a bird, banana, our girlfriend's hand. Accomplishing this one detail can do great things for your golf game. But, it takes a lot of discipline.

Go to the practice tee and start with a short club. Make some practice swings while thinking about softening your grip pressure as you start the downswing. If it feels loose, sloppy, out of control, no way you could hit a golf ball, you are probably doing it correctly.

It won't take long before you feel the difference, and see the difference. The resulting shot will be longer and straighter using much less effort than your old swing.

Your swing should feel easier, smoother, and the ball should stop going right so much. For the right-handed player this is easy to remember: TIGHT GOES RIGHT! For the lefty, tight goes left. Not as catchy sounding but you left-handers can remember this.

Give this a try—it works. A little practice on softening your grip pressure will pay off big time on your scorecard!

Control Problems? Get a Grip!

I have been coaching golf for a long time. I've worked with people through handwritten letters (that was a long time ago), over the phone, via email, and even used signals from across the golf course.

I've always had pretty good success with all of these methods, but there's one thing I really have to be 'hands on' for and that is the grip (no pun intended). There's something about getting people to hold a golf club properly that requires me to be there, molding their hands around the grip.

I feel so strongly about having a good connection to the club that I will try to explain my thoughts on the grip here. As with most aspects of the game there are different opinions as to how we should hold a golf club. Here is mine.

Most people learning the game, and even many long time golfers, put the club in the palm of their hand where they have lots of skin contact. Our brain seems to feel the amount of skin contact we have with the club equates to the level of control we have over it.

I subscribe to the idea that we hold things in our fingers, not the palms of our hands. Knife, fork, ball, pencil… Why not the golf club?

I like to cup the fingers of my left hand by bending the last 2 joints so the fingertips are pointing towards the wrist. Place the grip in this cup of the fingers, making sure only the fingers are touching the grip, none of the palm (fig. G-1).

fig. G-1

For a right handed player this is easiest to do with your left hand hanging naturally at your side and the club running across your legs in front of you with the head of the club somewhere near or to the right of your right foot (fig. G-2).

Then I feel like I'm wrapping my little finger around the grip, and finally put my thumb down a little to the right side of the grip so it is almost or just touching the end of the index finger.

The right hand will fit very nicely to the left hand if you do it properly. Look at your right thumb and see how it looks like a chicken leg, specifically the drumstick. The meaty part if the right thumb will fit perfectly on top of the left thumb. The key is to make it fit, not make it feel good.

All that's left is to wrap the fingers around the grip as best you can without disrupting anything you have done to this point. Check the lines formed by the thumb and hand. These lines should be pointing between your right ear and right shoulder (Fig G-3). If you overlap or interlock your little finger go ahead and do that. If it feels wrong, or at the very least not quite right, you are probably close to perfection.

fig. G-2

fig. G-3

I believe a grip change is the worst-feeling change I can bring to a student. But, you will adjust to a grip change quicker than any other change. And the benefits realized by a good grip include better hand action through impact resulting in longer, straighter shots.

Putting your hands on a golf club properly is not easy, and at first it won't feel good or 'correct.' However, a good grip is essential to playing better golf.

The Short Stuff

I have a lot of people tell me they are happy with their game, but when it comes to 'the short stuff' they don't have any idea of where to start. Once again, let's not make this harder than it is!

The short game, regardless of how short you are talking about, is not as difficult as we make it. The problem people have is that they seem to forget they have a golf club in their hands to help them with the shot.

Faced with a shot 20 yards from the green and over a bunker, what do you normally do? a) Hit behind the ball and chunk the ball into the sand in front of you, or b) Out of fear of doing a), you try to help the ball get airborne and end up hitting the ball right in the forehead?

In the case of b), the ball fires knee-high across the green and, generally, into some form of trouble on the other side. Odds are, you now have a similar 20-yard shot from the other side of the green, and a bad attitude about what will probably happen.

For a long shot we use a long swing. For a short shot we use a short swing, or think of it as 'a short long swing.' To accomplish this, start by beginning as you would for a typical long swing. When the long swing goes back to where the hands are about waist high, there is very little wrist cock. From this position, turn the shoulders smoothly so the hands come through to about waist high on the forward swing.

Now, the secret for playing these little shots is to stand more on your left, or forward, foot and keep more weight there for the entire swing. Use a narrower stance, with the ball position about at the left heel. The reason for this is you are standing on your left foot so the low point in the swing will be further to the left.

This little change in your setup will also give your swing a steeper angle when the club comes back to the ball, which is exactly what we want. It is this steeper attack that produces that high soft shot, over the sand and onto the green. You don't have to try to swing steeper, it happens automatically due to the adjustment in the setup.

I don't want you to automatically take a more lofted club when you are around the green. A good rule to use is, "Get the ball on the ground as soon as possible!" Less airtime and more ground time increases your odds of hitting a good shot.

Let's take that 20-yard shot over the sand we discussed earlier. If the sand were not there, I would be looking at the grass between me and the green. Short grass around the green is a great place to use an 8-iron, or a 7 or 6. Less airtime, more ground time. My score just improved by half a shot, simply by using a less lofted club.

The distance the ball goes in the air is controlled by the distance we take the club back. Waist high back to waist high forward may make a pitching wedge go 10 yards in the air, or 20, or 40. I can't tell you how far because the distance is specific to you. You have to learn how far it goes. Learn to feel it.

It doesn't matter whether you have to go high over something, low under it, or even out of the sand. Weight on the left foot for all of these shots. Control distance by the loft of the club chosen and length of backswing.

It takes some practice to have a good short game. It's not as much fun to practice but the short game is where the money is. A little practice will provide a big payoff.

And remember, your plan for the short game is how soon you can get the ball on the ground. Pick the club that will get the ball on the ground and rolling, stand on the left foot, and be smooth!

Now, go have fun and practice your short stuff!

Trust Your Feelings & Hit the Wrong Club

Have you ever been faced with a shot and had a strong feeling what club you should hit? That little voice inside tells you, *This is a nice 7-iron! Just smooth it up there right next to the hole.* Then your playing partner, with his GPS device, tries to help by telling you the exact yardage, which turns out to be an 8-iron. Now what do you do?

Most of the time you take the correct club, the 8-iron. Then, at the top of the backswing the little voice that told you what club to hit in the first place reminds you it is a nice 7 and you have an 8-iron in your hand. This means you'd better hit it hard—solid too. OOPS!

More times than not I will go with my first impression, my gut feeling, when it comes to club selection. A lot of people don't like this conflict of 'do I trust my eye or do I trust the yardage'? I like it when my eye and brain tell me what club to hit because now I don't have to spend all that time figuring out what club I hit 173 yards.

For me, I have found it's almost always best to trust my eye and the little voice in my head rather than automatically go with the yardage. Besides, 173 yards at my home course could be anything from a 9-iron to a 5, or even more, depending on wind and other conditions.

It's all about commitment. If you're committed to the club in your hand, EVEN IF IT'S THE WRONG CLUB, you are better off than if you have the correct club and don't feel good with it.

I hit the wrong club all the time and by golly when I pull the trigger with the wrong club I feel good about the shot. I feel like I stand a really good chance of hitting the ball close to the hole.

But when I have the correct club for the yardage and don't feel good with it I end up adjusting my swing to compensate for the lack of comfort or commitment in my brain.

I look at it this way. My brain is a lot smarter than I am. I figure it has already taken into consideration how I'm swinging that day; maybe I'm hitting it real solid and a little longer than usual, my uphill sidehill lie, wind, etc., etc., and calculated that into the feeling I had when I first arrived at my ball.

I'm a golf professional not a mathematician. Most of the time I don't like to count beyond 4 except sometimes when I'm playing a par 5. My brain is my caddie and it knows how I hit the ball, where my strengths and weaknesses are, and how I'm feeling that day. So when my caddie tells me to hit the wrong club, I'm usually going to do what my caddie tells me to do.

Trust your brain. It's probably a lot smarter than the one swinging the club!!

Sometimes It Takes a While

Sometimes, my monthly contributions to the *Arizona Golfer Magazine* come so easily I can barely type fast enough. Other months I labor for days as to what I should write about. This has been one of those tough months.

Then, this morning I got a call from one of my 'kids,' a 50+ kid, who has gone through a tough time with her golf in the past year. She used to shoot in the low to mid 80s, and then slid into a couple of bad habits that caused her to consistently score well over 100!

I won't go into detail as to what her problem was. I'll just say she made a move early in her swing that required her to make several adjustments just to make contact with the ball. All these adjustments made her swing very mechanical and forced, pretty much everything I don't want to see in a golf swing.

The problem with this move is it is by far the most difficult swing problem to correct. I told her from the beginning this was going to take a while. She could continue to play like she was, to which she replied, "Don't even say that," or plan on 3 to 12 months of work to get back to where she used to be. And, there was a very good chance she would be even better than she was.

Fast forward a year following a lot of creative drills, sweat, two steps forward one step back, lots of patience and no patience, and of course a lot of tears. After all, she is accustomed to being one of the best players in her area, not one of the best in the third or fourth flight!

About 4 weeks ago I got a message from her. She had shot 74 that morning on a tough golf course, with a triple bogey on the first hole! She was back. She sounded like she used to sound, positive and loving golf again. She had believed in what we were doing for a long time but it just hadn't completely come together for her until that day.

When she called this morning, 'LaDonna' let me know she had won her Club Championship yesterday, shooting 76-75-77. She said she is hitting the ball longer and more consistently than she ever has. And it is easy.

I've talked and written a lot stressing the importance of solid mechanics in the swing. Changes don't feel good but give them a chance. That's the importance of having discipline in your game. Set the bar high but be patient about reaching it.

There is no greater feeling than when it all comes together, when your swing is almost automatic, and effortless. Golf has finally become easy. Don't forget what got you there: your plan, your discipline. That is what is going to keep you at that level and continuing to improve.

When the wheels start getting a little wobbly get help early. Don't wait till you've run your game completely off the road and into the ditch. A little tune-up can save a lot of time and avoid the painful repairs that might otherwise become necessary to get your game back on the smooth road again.

Just Spray One Way

How much easier would the game be if you eliminated one, just one, shot from ever happening again? Which one would you get rid of? The top, the skull, the shank (sorry, most people don't like to hear that word), the chili dip? Forget it—I'm afraid we're all going to have more of these bad shots. But, what if you were to never hit a left to right shot again, or never had the ball turn left when you hit it; how much easier would the game be?

I was playing with one of our members about a month ago and he hit a solid drive off the first tee that fades gently to the right about 15 feet, stopping around 270 yards off the tee. His comment, "Looks like I'm playing a fade today." And he did, at least for the first 3 holes.

Then he was loosened up and started to draw the ball, which lasted for another 3 holes before his little draw became a full-blown hook with the occasional slice thrown in to really confuse his thought process.

After that, he did not hit another fairway the rest of the round. Why? He didn't have any idea of which way the ball was going to turn once it left the club. I asked him why he didn't put a little effort into eliminating one of the shots. It didn't matter which one, just make sure the ball goes straight or only turns one way. He said, "Sign me up!"

The next day we went to the lesson tee and in a short time established that his natural ball flight was either straight or moved a little from left to right. He had been fighting with the fade for some time because he had it in his mind that a fade was weak, and he certainly was not going to be known as a weak player. I reminded him of a few guys named Nicklaus, Trevino, and Couples who have done pretty well playing the fade.

Two days later he took his new thought process to the course and ended up having his best round ever by 4 shots! He did not miss a fairway to the left and only missed 2 fairways to the right. And the best part is, he realized when you fade or slice the ball into trouble you will generally need another fade or slice to get out of trouble and back on the course.

You need to have an idea of which way the ball is going to fly. It's pretty hard to swing a golf club with your fingers crossed in hopes of getting a good shot. The guy that stands on the tee, aims down the middle of the fairway, and declares he will never swear again if the Golf Gods will just let him hit the fairway, is moments away from swearing again.

It isn't that difficult to eliminate one shot from your game, you just need to figure out what your natural ball flight is and make a small adjustment so the other shot doesn't show up unless you want it to. If you need help sorting this out, tell your local PGA Professional you only want to spray the ball one way!

No Feel? Move the Ball

I'm sure you know how difficult it is to get all of your game working at the same time. One week we're saying, "If I could just get the short game working," and the following week it's, "Once I get close to the green I'm great—it just takes me a while to get there!"

It seems no matter how much we practice, or how much we believe in what we're doing, it is so rare that we ever get the long game, mid and short irons, and short game/putting all working at the same time.

And the most frustrating thing is, when you step on the first tee you really don't know what parts of your game are going to show up that day and what parts you are going to struggle with. No wonder the game drives us crazy!

I know when I get on the golf course most of the time I'm not really well prepared for the round. I don't have time to practice regularly, and when I do play I am usually running to join my group on the first tee. My warm-up seems to happen on the first couple of holes before I get a feel for what my body wants to do that day.

I know when I haven't loosened up my whole body doesn't function very well—my legs and lower back are tight which causes me to hit my first few shots to the left. So, I start my round trying to make good swings and hit good shots, knowing I am going to most likely pull the ball to the left. So, I aim a little to the right.

Then, as I loosen up and my swing feels better, I adjust my alignment so I am set up more towards my target. But what happens when I continue to hit the ball left, or right, or a little heavy or thin? Now what to do?

The first thing I do, when a particular aspect of my game is not quite what I want, is check my setup and alignment. Most people, myself included, tend to get too far from the ball at address. Combine that with poor alignment and there is no way the ball will go where we want. If the alignment checks out OK and my swing feels pretty good I will check my ball position.

The best way to do this is make a good practice swing and see where the club clips the grass. This is where the club wants to come down. Put your feet back where they were and then put the club down where it touched the grass.

This is where you want to position the ball for that club. Generally, you will find the club touches the ground closer to you than where you have been positioning the ball. It may also be further forward or back in your stance.

This is a little exercise I use all the time when I am practicing and playing. I like it because finding where the club wants to come down confirms good ball positioning and gives me the absolute best opportunity to produce a good shot!

In a nutshell, when your swing feels pretty good but is not producing, don't start tweaking your swing. Tweak your ball position. This should give you a sense—or feel or sensation—you can key on. A key that helps you swing more comfortably and produce better shots.

Why Do I Always...

I was talking with my friend Jack the other day and he asked me why it is that he plays the same holes poorly almost every single round. My response was, "I don't know Jack, why do you think you do that?"

He says, "I don't know. All I know is I'm going to hit one in the water on the right side of number 11. I've even gone to the far left side of the tee so I can get away from the lake, but then I think I pull across the ball and it slices about twice as much as normal and goes into the lake anyway."

"Jack, do we need to talk any more about this? I think you just answered your question."

Jack and I are having this conversation on Tuesday and he's not playing golf till Saturday, but he already knows one is going in the lake on 11 the next time he plays. He knows it today, he'll know it tomorrow, and he'll be thinking about it as he plays the first 10 holes on Saturday.

Jack already answered his own question when he said he pulls across the ball in an effort to keep the ball from going to the right. Pulling across the ball increases the sidespin on the ball, which makes the ball turn right even more than usual. Combine that with knowing he is going to go into the lake, and it becomes inevitable.

Watch the tour players when they need to slice a ball around a tree. Their swing path is more across the target line, or from the outside in, or from the right side of the target line before impact to the left side of the line after impact. AND, more importantly, they do not fully release the club, which keeps the hands from turning over. This is textbook for how to intentionally slice a golf ball.

More than anything else, a slice is caused by poor hand action. The slicer's hand action will always fall short of squaring the club at impact, generally because they are holding on to the club too tightly in an effort to control what it is doing.

If you want to avoid slicing your ball into the lake try this. Make a swing at a quarter speed, and after you get past the impact zone to where the club is about waist high on the forward swing, or parallel to the ground, stop and check where the toe of the club is pointed. I bet it is pointed to the right of your target line, or positioned so the face of the club is pointed somewhat up.

The correct position when fixing a slice would be to have the toe pointed up at the sky or even a little behind you. You may feel as though the back of the right hand is facing a little up to the sky as well.

Letting the club release will do several good things for your swing. Not only will you eliminate some, if not all, of your slice, but by releasing the club better you will generate more clubhead speed WITHOUT TRYING.

More distance with less effort! And, no more going into the lake on the right side of 11.

Hitting the Between Shots

I've had a run recently of people wanting help with their short game. More specifically, shots from less than 100 yards.

These were all previous students who initially came to me wanting to hit the ball longer and more consistently, but didn't want to mess with hitting short shots. Now they have seen the importance of the short game.

I watch them hit a few shots and very typically they are making a good shoulder turn with a full wrist cock, and starting the downswing with a weight transfer to the left side. All great stuff…for hitting the ball a long way!

Most people use their normal backswing and realize the ball is going to go way too far, so on the downswing they put on the brakes and try to slow the club down. This is like driving your car with one foot pressing the accelerator and the other on the brake. It doesn't work!

The key to hitting consistent shots of this distance is to first of all, eliminate all those things you do to hit the ball a long way. This is not a power swing.

It's a much more controlled swing that utilizes the larger muscle groups of the back and shoulders. The large muscle groups fire longer and more smoothly than the quick-firing smaller muscles in the arms and hands.

First, I want you to feel like your sternum, or breastbone, is swinging the club. Feel like you keep your hands in front of your chest when you swing. This will get the big muscle groups working.

Secondly, feel like you keep the grip end of the shaft pointing at your waist or belly button throughout the swing. Just smoothly turn the club back to about waist high and then turn through, finishing with the hands about waist high on the forward swing.

When you start to practice this shot DO NOT try to hit the ball at a specific target. You first have to get comfortable with the technique and then see where the ball goes.

This is mostly a flat-footed, upper body swing with minimal hand action. Be smooth and feel as though you are keeping the end of the club pointing at your body—not down at the ground. If the grip points at the ground you probably have too much wrist action.

Once you get the feel for the basic swing you can pay attention to how far the ball is going. That is exactly how far it should go. Now you can experiment with a slightly shorter swing, or a more aggressive forward swing and see how far the ball goes.

Try these shots with your different wedges, maybe even a 9- or 8-iron. Now you have a variety of shots you can use for those awkward distances that come up as you play.

Why Don't New Clubs Work Longer?

Have you ever bought a new club, or set of clubs, that work like magic for a while and then, before you know it, the magic is gone and they don't work any better than your old set?

About 6 months ago, after using the same driver for 8 years, I decided to upgrade to some new technology. I called my sales rep and told him a couple of specifications I wanted and had him pick the model he felt would be best for me.

When it arrived I took it straight to the first tee and played 18 holes with it. I couldn't believe how easy it was to hit. Time after time I hit these hard, solid drives with about 5 yards of draw, all going about 20 to 35 yards further than drives made with my old club. I hit all 14 fairways with it. I love technology! I'm starting to think about the Senior Tour!

Well, the honeymoon lasted for about 2 rounds and then the magic left. I didn't completely fall apart off the tee, I just didn't hit the ball as well as I did when I first pulled the club out of the box. Why does this happen?

I think all of us probably do the same thing I did. I hit the ball so well so easily. I didn't know my new club so I didn't try to do anything with it. I just gave it a swing to see what it would do. And when I stepped on the throttle to hit the ball a little further, it went further. Finally, I tried to hit it a little too hard and I almost hit the ball into another zip code.

New clubs and new technology are wonderful. We can hit the ball longer and straighter than ever before. Our bad shots no longer go into the bunkers around the green—they go a little left or right and just a few yards shorter than our good shots.

We begin to feel like we couldn't hit a bad shot if we tried. We begin swinging harder and we hit the ball further, until we swing a little too hard. Instead of making our normal swing we get carried away with seeing how far our new technology can hit the ball and eventually our mechanics break down.

Technology is a wonderful thing! It enables us to play better than we ever have and we get more enjoyment out of the game. But technology can only do so much. It can take a marginal shot and make it very playable. But, if you want to hit the ball further see your PGA Professional for some coaching. A few sessions can do things for your game technology could never do.

Imagine how good you could be if you combined technique with technology. You could probably hit the ball so hard... Never mind!

Leave the Club Alone

Last week we had a major figure from the Arizona sports world visit us here in Mazatlan. This was not the first time he had been here, but it was the first time I had the pleasure of playing golf with him.

Even if I hadn't known his athletic background it was obvious from his first swing he had great talent and awareness of what his body was doing. Unfortunately, as we all know, athletic ability is not always an asset when it comes to playing golf.

Over the years I've had the opportunity to work with many professional athletes and have found that some sports produce better golfers than others. In case you are wondering, hockey players are the best. They seem to have great awareness of what their bodies, and hands in particular, are doing.

Anyway, my 'Arizona Athlete' was very accomplished in two sports, one of which generally produced significantly better golfers than the other. This made watching his swing very interesting because I never knew which sport was going to take over. He didn't seem to either.

Athlete hit a lot of good, surprisingly long shots. And he hit some surprisingly short crooked shots. Obviously, he had received good coaching in the past, but the athlete in him kept taking over and causing problems.

Athletes tend to be a little bullheaded. After all we are athletes! And with the incredible God-given talent we possess it only makes sense we can figure out how to hit a golf ball. Heck, it isn't even moving. How tough could it be?

Finally, Athlete hits a solid 7-iron on a water hole that comes up about 20 yards short. Splash. He turns to me and says, "Why does that happen? I hit it solid but it doesn't go anywhere. What's the deal?"

I explain the best way to generate clubhead speed is by letting the hands release on their own! When the hands release properly we generate maximum club speed through the ball. When we try to generate a little extra speed by making the club go faster we are actually slowing the club down.

By trying to generate more speed we end up creating tension in the hands, arms, and upper body. The hands and club release too early and maximum speed occurs well before the club gets to the ball. No matter how solidly you strike the ball, the club just isn't going very fast, so the ball doesn't go very far.

I tell Athlete when he starts his downswing I only want him to think about relaxing his grip pressure—that's it! I throw another ball down, he relaxes his grip pressure, the ball flies to the back of the green, takes one hop and stops. Athlete says, "Wow, that's pretty cool!"

Your clubs are made to help you hit the ball. Leave the club alone. You've got enough to do just making good moves and letting the club do its thing.

A Weak Thumb Can Add More Power

Last week I was working with one of my regulars who, according to him, had "lost it completely! I think I'm doing everything right but I don't have a clue where the ball is going. I think you just need to start over with me!"

Mike is about a 10 to12 handicap, plays regularly, and practices a couple of times a week. I have worked with him 6 or 7 times over the last couple of years and he has become a more consistent player. He rarely has a bad day that is more than 2 or 3 strokes over his handicap.

I watched him hit a few balls and couldn't believe how inconsistent he was. Swing looked pretty good, but he couldn't play to a 20 handicap if his life depended on it. So what would cause such a consistent player to completely fall apart?

Turns out he had bad thumb. Not a bad thumb, not arthritis, not a sprain, just bad thumb position. I asked him what he was doing with his right thumb. He told me one of his buddies who hits the ball a long way has his thumb on top of the club, so he thought he'd try it. And, he said it did make him feel as if his swing was faster, more powerful.

I reminded him his buddy has to buy him a margarita 9 rounds out of 10, and plays to an 18 handicap.

When you swing a golf club properly it doesn't really feel powerful. That's why your brain is constantly trying to work something into your swing to make you feel stronger, more powerful. After all, if the ball goes that far with that smooth easy swing think of how far it could go if you put some testosterone into it!

It's important to understand that feeling powerful does not translate into being powerful. In fact, feeling powerful usually translates into 'I'm going to need a lot of balls today'! If you start feeling powerful you may want to adjust whatever is making you feel powerful to something that feels weaker.

I moved Mike's right thumb over to the side of the club so it touched the tip of his index finger. I warned him this was not going to feel good. He made a practice swing and fully agreed—it felt terrible.

"Now, hit a ball, but when you start the downswing and it feels really terrible and weak, don't do anything to make up for the weak feeling. Just hit a weak shot." He hit it great along with the next 5 balls. He was amazed that a small adjustment could make such a big change.

Although this small change of his thumb position didn't feel good at first it wasn't a big change. But, sometimes a small adjustment can cause other parts of your swing to come back into the proper sequence.

When you're having problems with your game don't assume you need a major overhaul. Sometimes it's as simple as moving your thumb half an inch.

Plan Your Play from the Green

I did a clinic before a couples event this week. Generally, I let the people determine what subject they want me to address. They decided they wanted to learn about Course Management, as long as that meant determining how to decide the best way to play each hole.

Great question! We all hop in carts and go to the first tee. I ask several people what they see, what their strategy is for playing their tee shot. Most comments were along the line of keep the ball right of the trees and left of the sand. This is a par 5 so I covered the second and third (and for some, the fourth) shots as well.

Some of the guys wondered what they should do if their second shot went to the left of the second dogleg onto the rolling mounds, leaving about 100 yards over sand to a narrow green. They weren't amused when I told them to go find it and hit it again, and don't go in the big deep bunker in front of the green.

Then I explained they needed to keep in mind golf course architects use terrain—sand, water, trees, rocks, anything they can get their hands on—when designing the hole. The purpose of utilizing all these elements is not just to define where the hole goes or make the course pretty, but to present a specific look to the players.

Much of this look is intended to play with the golfer's mind, to intimidate the player and make them see things that may not really be there. Architects are sneaky, nasty, sadistic maniacs who take great pleasure in messing with our heads.

I then take my 60 people up onto the first green and have them turn around and look at the hole from there. I hear a lot of mumbling. I ask where they think they should play their approach shot from in order to give them the best chance to hit this green.

Virtually everyone pointed at the wide spot at the second dogleg. "How far is that from the mounds to the left when you play the hole?" I asked. Most figured between 50 and 75 yards. "Then why would you be way over to the left in the mounds, hitting over the deep sand, to a narrow green?"

The guy who asked me about the mounds in the first place says, "I would be better off playing out of the right rough straight into the green than anywhere left, let alone in those hills where I usually am."

My favorite comment was, "When you play the hole it looks so narrow, but from here it's easy to see the fairway is really wide there." They got it. They understood why I had dragged them all the way out there.

It's OK to make your plan for playing a hole from the tee, but don't formalize it until you have stood on the green and looked back towards the tee. Oftentimes you'll see a completely different hole, and the easiest or most logical line to follow is more obvious when viewed looking back towards the tee.

COURSE MANAGEMENT

What's This Course Management Stuff?

THERE'S BEEN A lot of talk recently during the television broadcasts of the US Open and the British Open—sorry, make that the US Open and The Open—about course management. In my opinion, most problems people have on the golf course could be minimized if they just had some of this course management stuff!

I know most of my fellow golf professionals talk about it with their students. Almost every article I write deals with course management at some level, whether you realize it or not. So, why is it so tough to grasp what this is all about?

Let me put it this way—why do we try things like hitting a shot we know has little chance of succeeding, but we do it anyway? Is a golf ball really so powerful, so consuming, that it can cause an otherwise well-disciplined man or woman to make such foolish decisions? I'm starting to think it is.

We religiously feed the dog twice a day, the kids three times, change the oil in the car every 3,000 miles. But, when faced with a low-percentage golf shot our brain seems to say, *Go ahead—who knows, this might be that one time in a hundred that you actually pull it off!*

Course management is about knowing what you can and can't do, knowing your limitations, your ability. It's about keeping your emotions and pride under control. It's realizing that 9 times out of 10 you will have a lower score by playing safe and hitting a short iron beside the lake and then another one safely onto the green, rather than trying to hit a long club over the water.

We don't have to be mathematicians to realize that out in one, back in two, hitting three—or what I call counting by twos—is a lot harder on our score than counting by ones.

Let's go back to the two recent National Opens. The best in the world gave us great examples of both good and poor course management. We saw players try that low percentage shot out of long grass only to advance the ball a short distance and still be in the junk.

Immediately, you could see the pain on their faces as they realized the mental mistake they had just made, and now they essentially had the same shot again. By trying the hero shot they ultimately added two or more strokes to their score.

We saw many players take a short club and slash the ball only 50 yards or less to get it back onto the fairway, back in play. And, how many players actually hit the ball straight sideways or even backwards to hopefully get back in play because they knew it would be their best chance of avoiding a really ugly score on the hole.

As I've said before, we're not that good and golf is hard—really hard. Play within yourself. Play the shot you're capable of hitting. Play the shot you feel comfortable with. You may be surprised at how much better the scorecard looks at the end of the round.

Remember, the Hole Starts on the Tee!

The hole starts on the tee! It doesn't take a genius to figure that one out. But far too many people don't really pay much attention to what they're doing when they get to the tee box.

Grab the driver, march up to the tee, get somewhere between and behind the markers, and tee it up, giving little thought to the consequences of what you're doing.

When teeing your ball, your location side to side on the tee box can greatly determine how you are going to play the hole. For example, if your normal shot turns left to right you are probably concerned about the lake or out-of-bounds on the right side of the hole. The natural tendency is to get as far away from your problem as you can by teeing the ball up on the opposite side of the tee box. In reality, this is the worst thing you can do.

To help prove my point, draw two parallel lines on a piece of paper representing the left and right edges of the fairway. Next, draw the tee markers the same width as the fairway.

Now, from the left side of the tee draw a line showing the shape of your normal left to right shot so the ball finishes in the middle of the fairway. In order to land there, the flight of the ball must hug the left side of the hole or even pass over the left rough.

Next, draw a line from the right side of the tee box showing the same ball flight. The ball would start towards the left rough and then fade back to the middle of the fairway.

By playing your tee shot from the right side of the tee box, you are playing away from the trouble on the right. The ball is over the fairway the entire time and nowhere near the trouble on the right.

Play from the left and you are playing parallel to the trouble with the ball working or turning TOWARDS the trouble. The important thing is to determine where YOUR trouble is. It may not always be the obvious trouble.

There's a hole on my home course with a lake down the left side and nothing on the right but 5 acres of rough. The lake on the left is the obvious trouble. However, from the rough on the right my second shot is longer and into the prevailing wind. I make very few pars from there.

I tee the ball up on the right side of the tee and aim down the left side, towards the lake. I'm not worried about knocking it in the lake because I haven't done that for a long time. It's the rough on the right that scares me. Now I'm hitting the fairway most of the time and making a lot of pars.

Once I start hitting my tee shots into the lake I will adjust because my trouble will have changed from the rough on the right to the lake on the left! A good example of how your trouble can change over the course of a few rounds.

I've seen this one little tip save many people a lot of strokes. Give it a try. It can help you too!

Play to Your 'Personal Par'

I was playing with one of my members last week and on the third hole he didn't hit his tee shot very well, leaving about 210 yards over water to the green. He pulls out his 3-wood, makes a couple of practice swings while mumbling to himself and shaking his head, and then addresses the ball.

Now keep in mind this is a guy who, if he tees up a 3-wood and hits it on the button, might hit it 210 in the air. Hitting it off the fairway—no way.

I said, "Hey Ed, what are you doing?" He tells me it's the only club he has that gives him any chance of clearing the water. "Eddy, what are the odds of you carving your 3-wood off that thin lie and getting it across the lake?"

Ed steps away from the ball, looks at the lake, then back at his ball, and says, "Not happening!"

"Why don't you take an 8- or 9-iron and smooth it up there to the left of the lake, then smooth a wedge onto the green? Two putts, and you take your bogey and that new Pro V-1 on to the next hole."

Now here's the best part. Ed, who has played golf for more than 20 years, looks at me dead serious and says, "Can I do that? Is it OK, I mean, is it legal to do that?" Eddy, Eddy, Eddy. I'm starting to understand why he buys balls by the dozen.

I then explained the idea of playing golf to your "Personal Par." You may need to quit trying to hit your drives 250 yards, or carry a 3-wood 210 over water.

For example, if your handicap is in the mid to high teens, you are a bogey golfer. Look at each hole from the standpoint of where you can reasonably play each shot so bogey is easy and most likely the worst score you will make.

The 16th hole here at Estrella del Mar is a 212-yard par 3 from the back tees, playing straight to the ocean and into the prevailing wind. Three-woods and drivers are common club selections here.

Personally, I approach this hole as though it is one of those drivable par 4s you see on tour from time to time. If I manage to make 3, I feel like I made a "Personal Birdie" on the hole. When I make a 4 it doesn't tear my heart out, simply because this is a very difficult hole.

Before you play your next round of golf, take 15 minutes to analyze what you can realistically and easily make on each hole, and how you will play each hole to achieve that score.

For instance, plan on a 3-wood off the tee, then a 7-iron well right of the big tree, and an 80-yard pitching wedge to the green, making sure to leave the ball short of the hole. This should leave a fairly straight uphill putt, which should make a 5 the worst score you would make—Bingo! You have just eliminated making a double bogey or worse!

Once you figure your Personal Par and your game plan to shoot it, stick to it when you get on the course. You just might find this game is a lot easier when you have a plan to follow. And, it won't be long till many of those Personal Pars turn into Personal Birdies!

Fun Golf—What a Concept!

I was working with one of my members this week and he made a comment I really liked. Bill plays in our Senior Men's Group, handicap in the high twenties (or low thirties), and really just wants to eliminate the really costly shots, like when he chunks the ball 10 yards instead of hitting it 110 yards.

He is the shortest hitter in the Senior group and he's fine with that. As he puts it, "I just want to be OK at golf and have fun, hit some good shots, and not lose a bunch of balls."

I ask Bill if he ever addresses the ball and hears the little voice in his head say, *Billy Boy, what are you doing? You got no chance of pulling this shot off!*

Bill looks at me like I'm a mind reader. "Happens all the time!" We talked about some course management ideas like knowing his limitations, not trying the impossible shots, and tuning out his buddies who talk him into trying things he shouldn't.

He gets real quiet and then, finally, he says it. "You mean you want me to play fun golf?"

I love it—*Fun Golf,* what a concept! Instead of trying to hit low-percentage shots, losing balls, taking penalty strokes, and losing as much as 50 pesos a round (about $2.50 US), it's OK to play around the lake, which is what he actually does AFTER first hitting a ball into the lake.

Fun Golf. I know it's not for everyone, but for a lot of people it's a brilliant idea. For those who are just starting the game, and those who want more enjoyment on the golf course, it is a great approach.

When I worked in Colorado I had a member, George, who played 'Preferred Lies.' But his version of 'Preferred Lies' went like this: If you hit your ball into the woods and prefer it was on the fairway, you move your ball there. No penalty! Ball in the sand, no problem. That's why they put those rakes out there, to rake the ball out. Can't get over the lake? No problem; pick your ball up and carry it around! George was ahead of his time. He was playing Fun Golf 25 years ago.

So, how is Bill doing? He came by this morning and told me Fun Golf is the way to go. Any time that little voice in his head tells him *no way*, it's his reminder to save the ball and play smart. He now realizes how much all those penalty strokes have cost him.

He shot a 97 yesterday. The first time ever he has been under 100. Ever! You can still play by the rules and have fun. And, maybe even shoot your best score.

Fun Golf, Smart Golf. Give it a try.

How important is the Pre-Shot Routine?

One of my students asked me a great question the other day. She has played for many years and regularly shoots in the mid to high 80s. She said she felt a little silly asking me such a simple question and then inquired, "What should I be doing during my pre-shot routine?"

Here's what she told me her routine consists of. Stand behind the ball to get a feel for what she has to contend with: hazards, OB, how narrow the landing area is, and any other obstacles that may come into play. Approach the ball and make a practice swing, address the ball, and go through her checklist of what she needs to do to make a good swing. After hearing this I couldn't believe she plays as well as she does!

Sound familiar? I now understand why she stands over the ball so long before starting her swing. I have found most people tend to visualize things like, *I see the ball taking off low and then skipping 2, no, 3 times on the lake before it runs out of gas and sinks out of sight.*

Golf is a pretty tough game, especially if you only see the lakes, bunkers, and other things that run your score up. Odds are against you if you are concerned with the problems to the left, right, and center. AND if you have a feeling you are going to find one of the problems, you probably will. Her entire pre-shot routine focused on the trouble and not on anything positive

Time for a new routine. While standing behind the ball visualize your normal ball flight, landing safely exactly where you want it. Next, make a good practice swing. It doesn't have to be a full swing, just a good swing, keeping in mind the one or two swing keys you have been working on.

One last look at your line to pick out a spot a few feet in front of the ball that is on your target line. Move to the ball while taking a deep cleansing breath to relax your body.

Position the club to the ball so it is pointing at your spot, or intermediate target. Leave the club there and position your body to the club. If you have to look at your target fine, go ahead, but you don't have to because the routine you just followed has you all set to hit the ball at your target.

Once you have addressed the ball DON'T THINK! Pull the trigger as soon as you comfortably can so negative thoughts don't have time to enter into the process. Good thoughts rarely enter your brain while you are standing over the ball. The only thoughts you should have are the one or two swing thoughts you had for the practice swing.

I know this routine sounds long and drawn out in the beginning, and then rushed in the end, but it really isn't. It is a routine that will better prepare you to make a good swing, to let the club do the work for you, and to properly execute what you have been working on.

This will get your mind working on the positive, on what you want to do, on where you want to go.

So, how important is having a good routine? The day following our session she shot a 79—four shots better than her previous best! According to her, the pre-shot routine is more important than the swing itself!

The Mind is a Terrible Thing to Waste

How many times have we all heard that one? It may apply to a lot of areas of life, but I don't think it's ever more true than on the golf course.

How often have you been playing with someone who's having a good round and they say something along the lines of, "I'm playing out of my head," or, "I wonder when the wheels are going to fall off." With a thought process like that you won't have to wait long for your answer.

I was playing with one of my members who is about a 12 handicap. He's a pretty competent player, practices a lot and is a real student of the game. He just gets a bad attitude sometimes.

He starts out nice and relaxed and pars the first two holes, catches his wedge a little heavy on the third hole and dumps it into the lake and makes double bogey. On 4, using that same wedge from about 70 yards, he catches the ball right in the forehead and sends it about 140 yards into the Pacific Ocean.

The wedge receives a verbal lashing culminating with, "I hate this club and it hates me back. If I weren't so far from the clubhouse I'd quit right now."

On the fifth tee his normal fade turns into a snap hook, OB, heading for a triple bogey. He says, "Since I have to walk down 6, 7, 8, and 9 to get to the clubhouse I might as well keep you company and finish this 9. Then I'm done."

I love watching this. It is great entertainment because I have a pretty good idea of what's about to happen. Sure enough, after committing to quitting the game, that wedge he's not on speaking terms with knocks the ball 18 inches from the hole on 6, birdie. He makes another birdie with that same awful wedge, followed by a bogey and a par for a 42 for that side.

Not bad for a 12 handicapper that had a couple of meltdowns. All of a sudden he wants to play the back 9 because as he puts it, "I've found the secret. Without those couple of bad holes I was 1 under that side!" Okay!

You can imagine how the back 9 goes. The "secret" lasts about 3 holes and by the time we're on the 14th hole, as far as you can get from the clubhouse, he vows to quit again declaring, "This time I mean it."

He finishes with 3 pars and a birdie, for a 42-40, 82 on the day. The secret has returned and he can't wait to get to the clubhouse to see who is playing in the morning so he can show them—somebody, anybody—he has finally found the secret of golf.

I think we've all witnessed similar scenarios with people we play with and, unfortunately, most of us have actually lived this experience. The key is to learn from it.

When you think you've become mechanical, and mechanical just doesn't work. You can be mechanically perfect but if you are mechanical you will never produce the golf shot you are looking for. When you finally decide to quit golf, you quit being mechanical and let your body do what you've trained it to do.

Think of it this way: We are all pretty good with our own signature. Doesn't matter much whether you're using a $150-dollar pen or a felt tip marker, it is still your signature and looks like yours every time.

Now try your signature very slowly, making sure every loop and curve, every nuance that makes it your signature, is perfect. How does it look? Probably more like when you wrote notes from Santa to your children using the wrong hand!

Think during your practice swing. That's why it is called a practice swing. Think at the driving range. If you must think while playing, do so sparingly. Trust your body, and remember the mind is a terrible thing to waste. Especially on the golf course!

A FEW OTHER THOUGHTS

Savor the Small Victories

GOLF IS A very unique game. There's not much natural about it. From the grip through the entire swing there are very few elements that feel comfortable, let alone natural. We don't even look at our opponent, and if we do something the way the athlete in our brain tells us to do it, anything can happen, most of which is a long way from what we wanted.

Golf is made up of small, sometimes minuscule victories, sparingly scattered on the vast course of tragic mis-hits, ugly swings, mental lapses, bad attitudes, lack of discipline, unfounded experimentation… OK, you get it.

Golf's victories and landmarks are few and far between, but oh-so-wonderful when they happen. The first time you make it over the lake on 4, the effortless 6-iron that bounced once and stopped next to the hole for a tap-in birdie, the first time you shot under 90 'honestly' without any mulligans. It's the little things that are so big.

It took quite a while for me to grasp the idea that we never win, we never beat the golf course. The first time I played 18-holes without a bogey was quite an accomplishment, but only for a few minutes.

I played the first 12 holes bogey free and had thrown in a couple of birdies for good measure. On the 13th hole my tee shot went into the lake 294 yards from the tee. I didn't normally hit it that far but that day I did. I drop a ball, hitting 3, knock an 8-iron 2 feet from the hole and save my par 4 even with the penalty stroke. My thought was, the course only beat me by one that day!

My favorite story of 'the course always wins' came during a Mens Club competition between our course and a neighboring course. One of our players shot 66, a new course record at the time.

During the awards presentation I made a bit of a production to acknowledge Rich's accomplishment that day, listing the 6 holes he had birdied on his way to setting a new course record. Everyone gave him a standing ovation, congratulations and pats on the back all around. It was a great celebration of his performance.

When it was all over Rich called me over to his table and said, "Thanks a lot, it really meant a lot. But you know what? I had 64 right here," as he pointed to the palm of his hand.

In the 16 years the golf course had been open he had just played the best round of golf ever played there. And in his mind, as important as the course record was, he felt like the course only beat him by 2 that day. Still a pretty good day, but…

Golf is tough. Enjoy your time spent playing the game, the people you are with, and the good shots and accomplishments that happen, at some level, almost every time you play.

It's all right to never beat the golf course, but you can always have a few small victories.

Thoughts That Just Don't Work

There are several phrases or thoughts I hear a lot when I'm playing with my members or from the amateurs I play with in Pro-Ams. Some of these swing thoughts may have some merit, but others do a lot more damage than good.

For instance, *I need to keep my head down.* The only benefit I can see in thinking about keeping your head down is that you might keep your head somewhat still during the swing. The problem is, by trying to keep your head down, or still, the rest of your body becomes very still.

The golf swing is like a dance. There has to be motion to hit a ball, a lot of motion. A lot of proper motion. Take away the motion from your dance and all you have is standing still with an occasional twitch or jerk. Neither is good for dancing or golf!

How about, *Keep your eye on the ball?* The effect of this thought is about the same as *Keep your head down.* You are attempting to play a game of motion by restricting your movement. Very difficult!

If you need to keep your head or upper body quiet, try thinking about keeping the base of your neck still or quiet. The base of the neck is the center of the swing. Your shoulders are like the spokes on a wheel. The axle, or center of the wheel, stays still while the spokes and wheel turn around it. Same with golf.

This works very well, but only think about keeping the axle quiet on the backswing and then forget about it. If you bring the golf club down properly your head and neck will do what they are supposed to do. Don't worry about them.

Think about, *I need to finish my swing.* When people are trying to "finish their swing" it seems they are either trying to make the club move towards the target for an extended distance, or they are trying to finish with the club and/or hands high in the air over their head or shoulder or some other part of their body. Both of these moves are forced and they don't work.

Then there's, *I'm swinging too fast. I need to slow down.* Swinging fast is power and distance. This is good in golf. Most people should work on swinging faster. More club-head speed will make the course play shorter and therefore easier.

Now, if you mean you are swinging too hard and need to swing smoother, with less effort, then I agree. But please don't confuse swinging fast with swinging hard. Swinging fast produces long shots. Swinging hard produces errant shots and long, deep divots.

In a perfect swing, whatever that is, the club-head is moving at the target for only a millisecond, maybe for an inch or two. The swing moves the club on an arc from inside the target line, to the target line where it momentarily is moving towards the target, and then back inside and away from the target line.

This is the natural path of the circle, or arc, of the golf swing. To attempt to make the club do anything else is interfering with Mother Nature who, by the way, happens to be a golfer. Don't mess with Mother Nature—she will always win!

Beware of Technology

I had been out of town for about 2 weeks and had barely been home 10 minutes when I got an SOS message from one of my PGA LatinoAmerica Tour players. He tells me he's hitting everything great but his driver.

We get together the next morning and as he's loosening up he tells me a series of driver horror stories from the past 3 weeks. This one club has cost him about 30 strokes and, knowing him, at least a thousand dollars in his games with other players.

He starts with the wedges and works his way up to the longer clubs; all is good. He's doing exactly what we had been working on and effortlessly hitting solid shots that carry long with a little draw at the end. I don't see any reason he should have problems with any of his clubs.

He hits his 3-fairway-metal so solid it looks like it is going into orbit. Driver, four swings and I think he hit balls into three different zip codes. Time out. We adjust his setup which, for some reason, is substantially different from his stance with the other 12 clubs in his bag.

Five balls later I get him to stop working or manipulating the club throughout the swing and he looks like himself again. The problem now is his ball flight is starting to the right of his target line and then sliding right from there. Like it or not, at least we have some consistency. Then it hits me!

He's got one of those drivers where you can adjust all the angles into something like a hundred different combinations. And he likes to tinker with it. I ask my guy when he last adjusted the angles on his driver and he tells me a couple of weeks ago. Then it hits him! He looked like a cartoon character when the light bulb over his head turns on.

I love these new drivers that can be adjusted. Good swing or bad, anyone can adjust the club so they hit the type of shot they want. The problem is, people tend to fool around with their settings too much.

He had made an adjustment with his club and over the course of a few rounds it stopped working and he didn't change it back. Instead, he started adjusting his swing to compensate for his now ill-fitted driver.

I see this sort of thing a lot. The swing feels pretty good but the ball flight isn't what we want. Rather than check our basic fundamentals like grip, alignment, setup, or ball position, we tend to think our swing needs changing.

When your swing feels good and is producing a fairly consistent ball flight, even though the ball is not doing exactly what you want, don't blame your swing. Odds are the swing is fine.

It's your basic fundamentals that are causing the problems.

We Play Golf, and We Are Blessed

As I sit here trying to put together my contribution for this month's *Arizona Golfer Magazine*, it is a few days before Thanksgiving. By the time this edition comes out Thanksgiving will be a memory and most of us will be gearing up for Christmas and New Year's.

I'm looking out my window at a beautiful golf course, and beyond that is the beach and the Pacific Ocean. But my thoughts are a long way from anything to do with golf. I keep thinking about how lucky I am to live and work here. Happens every year about this time.

This past week I lost a special friend and favorite golfing buddy who died in a car accident. Two of my dearest friends I met at the first job I had in golf more than thirty years ago lost their young daughter to cancer. And my brother-in-law, Lyle, was moved into hospice care as his battle with cancer is nearing an end.

I've been feeling a little down for a couple of days, and as I walked the beach this morning I was reminded of how blessed I was. I was blessed to know these people. Each of them have had a big impact on my life. And the reason I know them is because of golf.

You learn a lot about a person when you play golf with them. Think about it. Watch how someone behaves on the golf course and you will have some very good insight as to how they handle their life. If they respect the game of golf, the field we play on, and the history of our game, I'll bet you that person has a good soul.

I've played many rounds of golf with these people. Standing on an elevated tee, gazing down the fairway of a spectacular hole, with 14,000-foot peaks of the Continental Divide rising up behind it, my brother-in-law Lyle once told me, "You know something? We play golf, and we are blessed." I felt this was quite a statement coming from a man whose 'church' had always been standing out in the middle of a pasture, gazing over his cattle.

I think we've all had those special experiences, one of those magical days on a beautiful course and just thought, *Wow, if I didn't play golf I would never have seen this view, felt this peace, and appreciated Mother Nature and the way the golf course architect worked with Her to make his design fit into Hers, seemingly without disturbing it.*

So, as we go through the holidays and the end-of-year assessments, office parties, family gatherings, resolutions, and everything else that goes with closing one year and opening another, I hope your view of this year is positive and you take from it a great outlook for the coming year.

And, I hope every time you are on a golf course from now on, at some point, you look at the beauty surrounding you and realize, *I play golf, and I am blessed.*

My brother-in-law, Lyle
"We Play Golf and We Are Blessed"

Tell Me What You Want

When I work with someone for the first time I like to find out a little about them: other sports they play, any physical issues they feel I should be aware of, and what they would like to accomplish during our time together. I recently learned that I need to make sure I understand clearly what their goals actually are.

For example, one fellow told me he would like to learn to hit fried eggs. For those of you new to this game, I should explain the term 'fried egg,' to a golfer, refers to when a golf ball lands in a bunker, or sand trap as it is frequently called, and it does not come out of the crater formed by its impact. The image of the ball sitting in the crater resembles a fried egg.

Anyway, with me eager to help him with his sand play we head to the practice bunker. I explain how the sand wedge is the heaviest club in the bag and is designed to bounce off of the sand, etc., etc.

We work on his technique for about 30 minutes and he seems fairly comfortable with being able to execute this shot. I ask him how he feels about his progress and he says, "Thanks for all the help with my sand game. I feel a lot better about it. But, when are you going to show me how to hit fried eggs?"

Somewhat confused, I asked what he meant by fried eggs. He replied, "You know, I want to hear the ball sizzle when I hit it."

You would think that that experience would be enough for me to never make that mistake again… but it wasn't. Recently, a woman said she would like to work on drawing the ball. I watch her hit a few balls and see she is a low handicapper who hits a nice ball with a little fade.

I explain what I would like her to do and why, she does it and the ball starts moving right to left in a beautiful draw. Since she is quite happy, and we have some time left, I ask if there was anything else she would like to work on. "Well, I'd still like to work on drawing the ball."

I immediately have a flashback to the fried egg experience several years earlier, and I start laughing. Turns out she had been a nationally-ranked curler in Canada. You know curling: it's where the players throw a 40-pound granite rock down the ice, team members sweep frantically, and there is a lot of yelling of directions to one another.

In the sport of curling, to 'draw' your rock means to lag it down the ice to a predetermined spot, frequently onto the bulls-eye at the opposite end. In other words, my student wanted to learn how to lag long putts close to the hole.

The moral of the story is, when you go for some help with your golf game make sure your coach really understands what you want to work on. Or, maybe this just applies to when you come to work with me.

The Myth That Just Won't Die

Years ago, golf professionals used to hear this comment all the time but I don't think anyone has said it to me for at least 10 years, probably more. I thought it was finally a thing of the past, until last week, when Frank dropped by and brought the old myth back to life.

Frank is a pretty good player, about a 6 or 7 handicap. He works on his game a lot and is always trying to improve. He's been stuck at his current level for a while and having trouble getting to his goal of a 5 handicap or less.

He believes he has found the reason he doesn't play better. And what would that be? Frank says, "I want you to teach me to hook the ball." And, why would that be? "Because good players hook the ball and bad players slice the ball."

Ohhhh Boy. I couldn't believe what I was hearing. We're talking about a guy who hits a beautiful little fade off the tee. It's a real thing of beauty. He probably averages about 290 off the tee, and I've never seen his drive do anything other than stay in the air a long time and then, when it starts coming down, slide to the right about 10 to 15 feet.

He is as close as I've ever seen to one of those mechanical golf machines you see on commercials from time to time. Never fails, long shots that slide a little right at the end, time after time. It's beautiful!

I explain to Frank I could get him to draw the ball but his handicap would probably go up because of the draw. He looked at me like I was crazy, which in fact I believe I would be if I changed his ball flight in the way he wanted.

Had he ever heard of Nicklaus, Couples, or a youngster named Dustin Johnson? Sure he had.

"Does Johnson play a fade?" he asked. Most of the time he does.

"Wow, he's long, too!" he realized. Yes, he is.

We all have our "natural" ball flight. Usually it is straight or slides a little left, or straight and slides a little right. It doesn't matter which one describes your ball flight, it is yours and you should learn to live with it. Trust it. Rely on it.

You want a swing you can repeat, which means a swing that produces a consistent ball flight. A ball flight that you can depend on when you've got a beer on the line with your buddies and only a couple of holes to play.

Trying to play a draw when your swing naturally produces a fade is just wrong. If your swing coach makes adjustments to your swing and you naturally start drawing the ball, great, play a draw and forget about fading the ball.

Golf is a tough game. Don't try to play an unnatural ball flight that just doesn't fit your swing. Lots of tour players fade the ball. It's OK for us to fade the ball, too!

My Group of Misfits

About once a month I will play the Saturday Skins game with a few of our regulars. It's a fairly diversified group of various abilities and personalities, but somehow we all hit it off and enjoy our competition and interaction.

One of the guys is an ex-golf professional who plays pretty well, but has a few quirks. Then we have Doc who, as it happens, is a doctor, carries an 18 handicap but plays like a 10. He hasn't missed a fairway in years but only hits the ball about 160 yards off the tee. He almost always gets up and down from anywhere inside 100 yards.

Our fourth player is Gino, a semi-retired real estate salesman whose biggest concern is whether we will finish each 9 holes before he runs out of beer.

The ex-professional is afraid of the hook so he opens the club face nearly 45 degrees at address, then makes some kind of gymnastic flip with his hands just prior to impact to get the club squared up. He never goes left anymore but does visit the OB right a few times a round. Then he asks me why that happened. Gee, I don't know! Your club is pointed way out there…!

Doc frequently wins. He wanted me to help him hit the ball farther. I got him hitting his tee shots about 200 yards for a while but now he's back to his old swing because he wasn't comfortable releasing the club. Said it felt like he wasn't controlling it anymore, which was the whole purpose for the swing change we made.

"Doc," I ask, "do you want to hit the ball farther or do you want to control your club?" I never get an answer from him. He still asks how he can hit the ball farther, and I still tell him to stop controlling the club so much; it knows what to do! He just laughs. Oh well, I tried.

Then there's Gino. I've worked with him for about 14 years, but only when we're on the course playing together. That is when he's not telling us we need to speed up because we have 3 holes to go on the front 9, and he only has 2 beers left in the cooler. He'll shoot anywhere between 78 and 105, depending on how cold the beer is.

Every time we're out Gino asks me what it is he needs to do to hit the ball better. Every time I answer Big Wrist Cock, Soft Hands. He says, "That's right, why can't I remember that?" I don't know Gino, I just don't know.

So why do I keep putting myself through this? This is my pack of misfits, my buddies. And the entertainment alone is worth far more than the 400 pesos (about $18 US) we play for.

We range in age from 48 to 74. We love the game of golf. We love each other. We hug when we get together and again when we part. This is one of my groups of friends. I love this game and the people who play it!

I think if you play golf there's a good chance you have a group similar to this. And, if you do, you are lucky!

Should Golf Be a Punishment?

It seems like most of the people I talk to at the end of their round are not very happy with their games. A few hours earlier they walked in, happy and optimistic about what their game would bring that day.

Now, they are complaining about how poorly they played, how expensive golf and equipment is, how their new technology worked great until they paid for it, then it didn't work any better than their old gear. They hate golf at the end of the round and frankly, it sounds to me as though people are looking for a reason to stop playing the game.

I've known people who have developed ulcers because of their golf games, lost sleep and lost appetites, you name it. They've tried shaving beards and mustaches, growing them back, new hairdos, new swing thoughts, shorter fingernails, good luck charms, good luck underwear… Come on!

Golf is a very difficult game. Difficult things can be frustrating. When Ben Hogan won the 1950 US Open he said he hit 4 perfect shots. In 72 holes he only hit 4 perfect shots. That's not very many for one of the greatest players ever who has just won the National Open.

What right do we have to let this game tear our heart out almost every time we play? You got that. We PLAY golf. Golf should be fun! Would golf be better as a punishment than a leisure activity? Sometimes I think so.

I have an idea. Instead of sending criminals to country club prisons where they have extensive law libraries, state-of-the-art computer facilities and exercise equipment, music programs, etc., etc., why don't we make them play golf so they can get the same enjoyment from the game we do?

What if you are convicted for robbery? You need to break 80 to be released. Commit murder and you have to shoot even par! Forget about getting your law degree or building up your muscles in the weight room. We should have the criminals participate in this fun game and let them play golf.

Just imagine the guy who's been in prison for many years, diligently working on his game in hopes of someday playing well enough to be released. He's having the game of his life, and only needs to make a 3-footer downhill that slides left to right to earn his "Get Out of Jail Free" card. What are the odds he will make it? Most of us have trouble making this when we're playing our buddies for a margarita!

I have a feeling laws will never change to where a prison release is dependent on a person's golf game. I have a feeling I will never be imprisoned and GET to play golf everyday. I have a feeling we will spend the rest of our lives struggling with the game we love and hate, can't beat and can't quit, lose sleep over and can't sleep without.

THE SWING

THE FOLLOWING SECTIONS are directed to the right-handed player. Left-handers should change the wording to the opposite side of the one I have referenced.

There are many opinions as to how we should swing a golf club. Weight 60% on your right foot, keep your head down, left arm straight, eye on the ball, focus on a single dimple on the back of the ball, turn your body away from the target, transfer weight to the left foot, turn your body toward the target, swing inside out, extend towards the target, finish the swing, high follow through, finish facing the target, hold that position till the ball lands. The last point is very important if someone is trying to take your picture for an action shot!

That's just the short list I hear most frequently. Are we really expected to do all this in the 1 to 1-1/2 seconds it takes to make a swing? No wonder people have so much trouble hitting the ball!

I'll be the first to tell you golf is a difficult game. But, it's not as difficult as we make it. Here is my take on the golf swing.

First, you need to have a good connection to the club—The Grip. I won't go into it here because we are talking about the swing, which assumes you, for better or worse, are already holding the club. For my thoughts on the grip go to *Control Problems? Get a Grip* in the Playing section earlier in the book.

Golf is not a natural game. If you swing a golf club the way your brain tells you to, you're probably going to have limited success. Here are some key points that tend to add to the difficulty of hitting a golf ball:

Unlike most sports, you don't face your opponent in golf. Just an FYI, the layout of the golf course is your opponent, not the golf ball. The ball is on your side. The ball wants to fly long and high and straight, and land next to the hole. The ball is like a puppy. It wants to please you. You just need to know how to talk to the ball, how to work with it.

During the process of swinging, a fraction of a second before the attack you have your back turned to your opponent. Nothing natural about that. Maybe that's why so many golfers attack the ball so violently. At least you can see the ball, so why not, I guess?

Most golfers realize, or at some level believe, a golf swing is a circular motion, in that all the moving parts—hands, arms, and body—basically move in an arc. This arc, or portion of a circle, turns around a central axis, the spine.

Imagine the base of your neck is the center of the wheel. Your shoulders are the spokes of the wheel, turning around the center. This is mostly true, with one exception: The arms appear to move in a circle, but they actually move up and down on a vertical plane. The only thing that makes it seem like they move in a circle is that they are attached to the upper body, which definitely does move in a circle, or arc.

All that being said, it really is pretty easy to swing a golf club. Follow with me and don't attempt to strike a golf ball for a while.

Let's get the long-winded more technical part out of the way so you can start working on a better swing and gaining more enjoyment from the game. This part lacks entertainment value, but knowing some things about the swing will help your problem-solving forever.

Following are my thoughts on the golf swing.

The Address

Golf is a sport. Fortunately, you don't have to be overly athletic to play golf. You just need to be able to move. Basically, I want to see a little flex in the ankles, knees and hips, with the knees over the toes. This is an athletic stance used by all athletes.

Bending at the hips tilts the upper body forward which enables the player to swing the club down to the ground where the ball is. Bending at the hip joint results in better posture that will help keep the back and spine fairly straight, rather than rounded as when bending at the waist. This is preferable for golf.

The arms and hands should hang down from the shoulders, with a slight reach towards the ball. For most people the hands will be about four to six inches from their body. This will vary depending on the player's height, posture, and body type. I don't want to see a big extension or reaching out to the ball with the hands and arms. Stay close to your work.

Tip: When you address, or position yourself to the ball, I want you to feel relaxed, with your weight a little more on the balls of your feet, and slightly more weight on the right foot.

The Arms

As I mentioned earlier, the arms and hands move up and down. To get a feel for the correct motion, address a ball (real or imagined) and just lift your arms up in front of your body so the hands are about waist height. Now, move your arms back to the starting position where the club would rest on the ground. This is what the arms do. Pretty simple!

Tip: Practice this until you are comfortable with it; 2 or 3 times should do it.

The Hands

The hands are a great source of power and will function perfectly if you leave them alone and don't try to make them do anything. For many players this can be the most challenging part of the swing.

Once again, lift the arms up in front of your body so the hands are about waist high (Fig 1). Now, cock or bend the wrist joint so the club moves towards your head (Fig 2). The club will be about head height this point. The left wrist and lower arm are nearly straight, or flat.

A slight 'cup' or bend of the wrist moving the knuckles to the left (Fig 4) is fine. A bend of the wrist to the right where the fingers are more visible is not acceptable (Fig 5). Please don't get started doing this. This position can cause injury, produce very erratic shots, and be difficult to correct.

Here is a good exercise to get the hands and arms working properly. Repeat the exercise you just did lifting the arms in front of you, and cock the wrists so the club moves towards your head. Now, turn your left shoulder in front of, or slightly below your chin, keeping the left arm fairly straight (Fig 3). This should put the club in a good position.

For now don't swing through at an imaginary (or real) ball. You are just working on getting comfortable moving the arms and wrists properly for the backswing.

Tip: Practice this until you are comfortable with it. Initially it probably won't feel natural or correct but you will get it in a short time

Fig 1   Fig 2   Fig 3

Fig 4   Fig 5

The Upper Body

Now we start the circles. A good upper body turn will happen by rotating, or turning, the upper body so the left shoulder turns in front of or somewhat under the chin.

As the upper body turns, the arms make their vertical move and the wrists cock so the club is close to a 90-degree angle from the left forearm, like we just practiced. It may feel like the hands are over or near the right shoulder, which is fine.

A good checkpoint is to stand next to a mirror or glass door so your reflection is to your right. Make your backswing or shoulder turn and stop at the top or end of the backswing. Now look at your reflection. The left arm should be on about the same angle as the shoulders, so the left arm appears to be angled between the head and right shoulder.

If you have done this properly along with a good wrist cock position, the club is roughly parallel to the ground and pointed towards your target. This position depends largely on your flexibility, so don't worry if the club does not get to parallel. If the club is short of parallel it will be pointing upwards and to the left of the target.

Tip: Practice this until you are comfortable and can get the hands and club in good positions at the top of the backswing.

NOTE: You release tension to hit the ball. You don't create tension to attack or strike the golf ball!

Tip: Face your mirror or window. The only thing to check on the backswing is make sure the right hip stays over, or to the inside of, the right foot. We don't want it to slide to the right or outside the foot. Practice this until you are comfortable with it. This move will create considerable tension on the outside of the right thigh. This is good tension.

Now take a break, and a deep breath.

OK, that is the backswing. I know at this point your brain may be getting full. I just gave you a lot of information. If you take it a step at a time it won't take long to feel comfortable with your golf swing. And, if you have played golf, much of this may already be second nature for you.

NOTE: I am writing this so it covers just about everything. The beginner can get started on the right foot, so to speak, and not get lost or develop a bunch of bad habits. If you have played some, this will simply be a guide or checklist for you when problems come up.

The Lower Body

During the backswing, when the upper body does its move correctly the left hip will be pulled somewhat in front of the body. This is not something you should have to think about, it happens because of what the upper body is doing.

Bringing the golf club from the top of the backswing to the ball is where things can get exciting. There is a tendency to forget everything we have learned and practiced, and our one thought becomes, *I'm going to punish this ball like it has never been punished before!*

At the top of the backswing, there will be a lot of tension in the left shoulder and upper left part of the back, on the outside of the right thigh, and possibly in the muscle running in front of the right hip into the groin. This is great! You have wound up the spring. This tension translates into power. This is good tension.

It is extremely important to remember the hands provide maximum power, if you have soft hands. However, power is useless if released or generated at the wrong time, which is what most golfers do. Because we naturally try to hit with the hands all our energy is spent before the club gets to the ball.

Now is when the lower body is of the greatest importance. The downswing must be initiated below the waist. Start by rotating (still using circles) or turning the lower body as if you were trying to point your belly button at your target. Or, point your right knee at the target. Or, turn left. Use whatever is the least cumbersome move for you to do to get the downswing started below the waist.

Done properly, the upper body will rotate (more circles) and the shoulders unwind to where the right shoulder is moving close to the chin, and the hands are about waist high. The wrists will still have most of the cock, or 90-degree angle from the forearm to the shaft of the club, as there was at the top of the backswing.

This is where physics takes over and the rest happens automatically. The power of the hands has been maintained to this point, and now releases the club naturally through the ball, as long as you have maintained soft hands.

Tip: Practice this exercise a lot! Focus on the lower body initiating the downswing, and light grip pressure, so you let the club get to the ball on its own. Do this several times, then do it several more times. This may become your most used practice tool. As usual, it won't feel natural at all but you will get it with a little practice.

Soft Hands

Remember I mentioned earlier that the hands and wrist cock were a great source of power? This is where it happens. The hands will work perfectly every time if you let them. The key is to let them. I talk a lot about Soft Hands. Soft Hands are a major key to a successful golf shot.

To feel Soft Hands, let's start with a baseball swing. Most of us played some baseball growing up so this should be fairly simple. The baseball swing is basically a golf swing only higher.

Loosen up like you are ready for the pitch. Here it comes. You start the swing by turning the lower body towards the pitcher and the arms and hands follow. If all goes well, the ball and bat run into each other.

Let your swing continue on past contact with the ball. Feel how the hands release and turn over? This is power. The cool thing is this release of the hands to and through the ball happens automatically. You don't have to make it happen, just let it happen.

Now, make some baseball swings at a normal speed. You should feel the hands and club release, or speed up, as the club swings through the area where it would be hitting the ball. You aren't making the hands release, you are letting them release on their own.

Here is an exercise to help feel the correct hand action. Put your hands in front of you about waist high, left palm down, right palm up. Now, at the same time, turn your left palm up and the right palm down. Repeat a few times. Not that tough to do.

Next, bring your hands together like you are holding a club. Without a club, mimic the golf swing and let your hands do the same thing.

This is power. This is how power hitters in baseball hit the ball hard, and far. And, this is how golfers should hit the ball.

The best part is, this will happen on its own if you have Soft Hands. Hold the golf club tight and you'll hit the ball all over the place and have no idea where it is going.

Be gentle with your grip pressure, use Soft Hands, leave the club alone, and you will stand a chance. No guarantees, but this will give you the absolute greatest chance to produce a good shot! Period!

Getting a Ball Involved

When you are comfortable with all these positions and movements you will be ready to introduce a ball into the process. Put the ball on a tee so the ball is about 1/2 inch off the ground. For now, always use a tee!

When you get a ball involved it's easy to focus on the ball and forget about what your body is doing. Hitting a golf ball is a result of making good moves. I don't care if you hit the ball or miss it. I care about you looking good. Make good moves. Look good.

If everything has been done, even just somewhat according to plan, you have a chance of at least wounding the ball. However, if you miss the ball it is not a problem. At least 95% of new players (and many experienced golfers, too) miss the ball their first swing or two.

I almost forgot. To answer your question about how long you use a tee? Until you don't need it anymore, or until you get tired of bending over to tee the ball up.

Tip: Hitting the ball is not the objective. Looking good is! Remember this!

If you look good I can help you. If your swing is a fundamental mess, we have to improve your fundamentals, or make you look good, before you will have any consistency.

The Swing in Pictures

Putting It All Together

Way back at the start of this section I listed the 15 most common thoughts people have when swinging a golf club. There is no way anyone can begin to make much of a dent in this swing checklist.

So, how in the world do we do all the right things, when we really just want to hit the ball and have some fun?

I can guarantee you won't be happy for long just hitting the ball. You'll want it to go higher, longer, straighter—something more than what you are currently doing. Golfers are not happy with just hitting the ball.

What do we do? It just so happens I know what to do. I know how you can have a better chance of hitting the ball more consistently and have a lot more fun while you're at it. It's called The Plan.

THE PLAN

I AM A huge believer in having a Plan. You can get away with a lot of imperfection if you have a Plan.

People, at some level, have a plan for everything they do in life. Why not for golf? A Plan will at the very least give you a chance to succeed.

Your Plan will contain a couple of elements of all those swing components I have previously talked about. How do you choose which ones you will use? When you were practicing, what was your thought to get to the positions or moves we wanted? The positions, or thoughts that worked will be your Plan until another thought works better.

Here are some examples of frequently used Plans:

- Head still, belly button (to the target).
- Left shoulder (to my chin), right knee (to the target).
- Create tension (in my left shoulder), Soft Hands.
- Hands over my (right) shoulder, turn left.

These are all common Plans. Notice each plan only has 2 parts: One for the backswing, and one for the downswing. One, Two. That's it.

A Plan is a flexible instrument, constantly changing. It may change from one day to the next or sometimes one hole to the next.

If you're having trouble with the backswing, review that section and find a thought or drill that works for you. That becomes the One in your Plan! Combine your new One with a thought that helps your downswing and you have your new One, Two. Your new Plan.

People who have a Plan quickly become much more aware of what their body is doing when they swing. They feel their hands get tight on the downswing. Or, they may feel they were flat-footed and didn't make a good move to the left side when initiating the downswing. Now they can fix the problem for the next swing.

You no longer need hours on the range and thousands of balls to fix your game. Just tweak your Plan and you're back on track.

When my students really put their Plan to work and understand how to adjust it, I will have worked myself out of another job. That, I honestly believe, is my job!

THE 19TH HOLE

I AM HOPING you are here because you read your way to this point and didn't skip here to put yourself out of the misery you were experiencing.

In an effort to make this educational, with a little humor mixed in, I hoped to use my years of coaching experience to help other golfers get a better understanding of what happens when you stand by that little white ball, moments away from sending it on its way, hopefully somewhat towards your target.

There is a lot that can and does happen when you swing a golf club. Once you accept the fact that your brain doesn't really know much about golf, you will be on your way to having a chance for success. No guarantees, but now you can at least start reprogramming your brain and begin the journey towards success with your golf.

The way I see people benefitting most from this book is to read it. Then read it again. The section on *The Swing* is most important because it explains how the body moves and how the various components of the swing work together.

Does your swing feel pretty good but gets a little jerky, or awkward, about the time the club gets to the ball or shortly after impact? If you can't figure out why, go to *The Swing* section. Somewhere between *The Arms* and *The Lower Body* you will find your fix, along with exercises to work on when you are practicing and playing.

I want this to be a tool you can use as long as you play. When you have problems, the answer is here. The more you use the book the less you will need it. In a short time, you will get to the point where you can fix your swing before the next shot, based on how the ball flies or what your swing feels like.

You have a Plan that will change from time to time. Your Plan is determined by which areas of the swing you are focusing on improving at the time.

Frequently, when I have worked with someone for a while, I will tell them, "I don't know if this crap really works or not. But, I do know if I can take your mind off the ball you will play a lot better."

As it turns out, I do know it works. Does it work because we are swinging better, or because we aren't thinking about the ball?

Does it matter?

Better Golf-How to Get it and How to Keep it.